When Less Is More

Using the Mind to Exercise the Body

(with notes for those with "Special Needs")

by Arieh Lev Breslow

Almond Blossom
PRESS

When Less is More: Using the Mind to Exercise the Body
© 1999 By Arieh Lev Breslow
First Printing 1999

All rights reserved. No part of this book may be reproduced
in any form or by any means, electronic or mechanical, including
photocopying, recording, or by any information storage and
retrieval system without permission from the publisher.
Almond Blossom Press, P.O. Box 10600, Jerusalem, Israel

Warning: The exercises in this book are gentle and most people can do them without harm. However, consult a physician if you have any outstanding health problems before you try the exercises in this book. The following instruction and advice are not intended as a substitute for professional medical counseling or treatment. Therefore, the author, publisher and distributors of this book disclaim any liability or loss in connection with the exercises and advice therein.

Library of Congress Cataloging in Publication Data
Breslow, Arieh Lev.
When Less is More: Using the Mind to Exercise the Body / by Arieh Lev Breslow – 1st ed.
1. The Middle Path. 2. Health. 3. Self-improvement. 4. Meditation. 5. Exercise.
ISBN 0-9644730-1-1   98-074463
                                                      CIP

Graphic Artist: Benjie Herskowitz
Illustrator: Avi Katz
Model: Anne Breslow

Printed in Israel

If you believe that you can do damage, then believe that you can repair.

Rabbi Nachman

Life is like shopping in a supermarket.
You can choose whatever food you want.
But remember,
When you get to the cash register,
You've got to pay for it.

Anonymous

Who can find a good wife?
She is more precious than rubies.
Proverbs 31: 10

To Anne,
for her love and support

Other books by Arieh Lev Breslow:

Beyond the Closed Door: Chinese Culture and the Creation of T'ai Chi Ch'uan

Acknowledgements

I thank the many people who contributed to the writing of this book. Fong Ha taught me the value of 'Standing Meditation.' Many years ago, Rabbi Bert Jacobson led me on a journey to find my 'spirit guide.' Ken Cohen, my first T'ai Chi teacher, set up the workshop where I learned the animal forms. Pardes Institute of Jewish Studies and particularly Bernie Steinberg introduced me to the writings of Moses Maimonidies.

Linda Chase Brody influenced my work with people who have 'special needs.' Her workshop and video were invaluable to my growth in this area. Dalia van Coevorden offered me the opportunity to work with a wonderful group of senior citizens. I leaned heavily on her wisdom and experience in the field.

I would also like to acknowledge Sherry Mandel who edited this book. She knew where to cut, how to streamline and, most importantly, played the devil's advocate. Her advice was priceless. Sally Oren and Danny Loney read the manuscript and offered incisive suggestions and criticisms. Esther Rosenfeld saved me from certain embarrassment with her proofreading skills. Michael Tobin's creative input provided the final proof that 'less is more.'

My wife Anne, who served as the model for the book, helped with correcting and simplifying the exercises. Without her practical knowledge and sharp eye, they would have been confusing and impossible to follow.

I want to thank Jean Naggar and Anne Engel for their helpful suggestions regarding the book's concept and structure.

I am indebted to my students who often served as unwitting subjects for my experiments as I searched for the right teaching methods. I am sure that there are many others whom I have left out due to an oversight of memory. I want to apologize to them all and offer my deepest gratitude.

Finally, 'the buck stops here.' I take the full responsibility for any errors in the text or the exercises. I hope that they are insignificant so that you, the reader, will easily find your way to The Middle Path.

Pictures and Illustrations

1. Maimonides   p. 12

2. Special Needs Class   p. 40

3. Picture of Cheng Man Ch'ing   p. 41

4. Nature Scene   p. 53

5. Correct Posture   p. 58

6. Abdominal Breathing   p. 65

7. First Posture Standing Meditation   p. 91

8. Second Posture Standing Meditation   p. 91

9. Third Posture Standing Meditation   p. 92

10. The Author and His Wife Doing Pushhands p. 100

11. Baby Smiling   p. 103

12. Ch'i Kung   p. 132

Contents

Introduction i
A Word about "Special Needs" vi

Chapter 1: The Wisdom of The Middle Path
    1) Growth of Extremism 1
    2) The Economic Roots of Societal Dis-ease 3
    3) Wants and Needs 5
    4) Foundations of The Middle Path 7
    5) Physical and Mental Health According to The Middle Path 11
    6) Diet and The Middle Path 15
    7) Exercise and The Middle Path 18
    8) Summary 20
    9) Practical Exercise – A Change of Mind 21

Chapter 2: A Warm-up for The Middle Path
    1) Introduction 25
    2) What's Different about this Warmup 27
    3) The Warm-up 29

Chapter 3: Meditation, Science, and The Middle Path
    1) Taming the Wild Horses 41
    2) Meditation and The Relaxation Response 42
    3) Meditation and The Middle Path 47
    4) Practical Exercise – Finding Your Internal Compass 53

Chapter 4: The Seven Steps to Better Health through Meditation
    1) Preparation 56
    2) Posture 57
    3) Focus 59
    4) Breath 62
    5) Centering 66
    6) Letting go 67

  7) Visualization 70
  8) Summary 72

Chapter 5: Meditations and Visualizations
  1) Introduction 73
  2) Sitting Meditation 74
  3) 1st Exercise – Counting the Breaths 74
  4) 2nd Exercise – Focusing 75
  5) 3rd Exercise – Using the Mind's Eye to Relax the Body 76
  6) The Importance of Doing Less 85
  7) The Virtue of Uselessness 86
  8) Summary 86

Chapter 6: Standing Meditation: Rooting the Body, Balancing the Mind
  1) Introduction 88
  2) Preparation 90
  3) Visualization 92
  4) Special Needs 94
  5) Summary 94

Chapter 7: Help for the Soul
  1) The Forgiveness Meditation 95
  2) Coping with Fear and Anxiety 97
  3) Coping with Pain 99
  4) The Smile Meditation 101
  5) Special Needs 103

Chapter 8: Strengthening your Ch'i: Two sets of Chinese Ch'i Kung
  1) Introduction 104
  2) Special Needs 107
  3) 1st Exercise – The Eight Pieces of Brocade 108
  4) 2nd Exercise – The Animal Forms 117
  5) Helpful Hints 132
  6) Summary 133
  Afterword 134

Introduction

There was temperance in eating and drinking. Their hours of rising and retiring were regular and not disorderly and wild. By these means the ancients kept their bodies united with their souls, so as to fulfill their allotted span completely, measuring unto a hundred years before they passed away.

Ch'i Po in "The Yellow Emperor's Classic of Internal Medicine"

I have a great job. I teach Chinese health exercises to people from all walks of life. I have taught T'ai Chi, Ch'i Kung, meditations, visualizations and various warm-up exercises to dancers, athletes, businesspeople, cancer patients, and the elderly. Daily, I teach my students how to relax, to improve their posture, to breathe properly and to strengthen their bodies' musculature. My work allows me to safeguard my own health while contributing to the well-being of others.

I have been fortunate to have a positive impact on my students' lives. Recently one of my students, a man in his seventies, whom I had not seen in several months, phoned me. He began with the words: "I owe you a debt." Debt, I thought, he probably forgot to pay for some classes. Then he told me some startling news. He had just been operated on for a brain tumor and was undergoing radiation him through the operation and recovery. They gave him something to focus on during a time of terrible uncertainty. He explained that it was a 'debt of gratitude' that he owed me.

This book is based on my experience of over twenty years in the health field. It is intended to help ordinary people to improve their health and to reduce stress through easy-to-learn exercises. Moreover, I have placed this health regimen in the context of The Middle Path, an ancient philosophy of sensible living, and demonstrated how it resonates with the findings of modern medical research.

The Middle Path, which I will discuss fully in Chapter I, is a time-honored way of wellness and well-being. It is a philosophy that emphasizes balance and harmony in the daily choices one makes. The Middle Path is so simple and obvious that it is often overlooked. In most cases, what is needed to improve one's health is a moderate and gradual change in lifestyle with a view toward the future, not a major overhaul of who we are as individuals. In most cases, the latter approach will only appear to work in the short run. The ideas of The Middle Path are the philosophical moorings to which I have anchored the practical initiatives of this book.

The various meditations, visualizations and exercises in this book are easy to learn. They are composed of only a few postures and focus on combining gentle movement with the breath. The exercises do not require exorbitant fees, special clothing or equipment. They can be practiced in a small place, almost any place that is quiet and where the air is fresh. All one needs is the will and perseverance to learn and do the exercises regularly.

They are also readily accessible to Westerners because many of them are part of the Western tradition. The reader will encounter the 'forgiveness meditation,' which comes from the Judaic-Christian tradition. On the other hand, I drew many of the focusing and breathing exercises from Eastern sources. As a Westerner who teaches an Eastern discipline, I have felt most comfortable when I could integrate the wisdom of East and West. Both cultures have much to be proud of. I believe that the 'twain' meet along The Middle Path, in the universal hopes and the shared dreams of most people on earth.

As a teacher, I have striven to be pragmatic, to pick and choose whatever works best for my students. Over time, I have not hesitated to experiment, retaining the successes and discarding the failures. This book reflects the distillation of this the successes and discarding the failures. This book reflects the distillation of this pragmatic approach and what I believe is possible for most people to learn from a self-help book. I have not tried to cram every meditation or exercise for every malady known to humankind into this book. Moreover, I did not design 'When Less is More' as an encyclopedic reference guide. It is not an attempt to be all things to all people. I have sought to emphasize quality in contrast to quantity. As an author proffering practical advice, my satisfaction will come from a book tattered from overuse rather than one intact but gathering dust on someone's shelf.

An essential feature of this book is that it stresses quality over quantity. In modern society, we frequently think that the biggest or the most is the best. Recently I heard a commercial on the car radio that emphasized 'more' of this and 'more' of that in a pitch to sell the product. The creators of the commercial had made use of the popular wisdom that equates quantity with quality.

But 'more' does not necessarily produce the results that people expect and can even prove to be detrimental. For example, we read about major corporations scaling down their work force and their business objectives. They are seeking to be lean and agile to better cope with a constantly changing world. The computer industry reflects this new reality.

This is also true with respect to the health of individuals. Bulging muscles are not a guarantee of health, nor is running several miles each day. Recent scientific studies have shown that a brisk twenty-minute walk produces all the aerobic exercise that most people require. It will surprise many people to learn that the simple act of standing in meditation is incredibly invigorating and healthy. It will astonish others to read about the scientific evidence that points to the positive influence on health when physical exercise and conscious awareness are combined. In other words, improving one's health depends on the quality of what one does and not necessarily the quantity. This is the way of The Middle Path, doing less and achieving more.

The practical exercises and techniques in this book will be of little value unless practiced within the broad context of the The Middle Path. They will be effective only if the reader adopts a lifestyle that promotes wellness and well-being. If someone meditates with the purpose of reducing stress and then does not alter a stressful and unhealthy lifestyle, his or her meditation will be of little help. Similarly, if a person who has suffered a heart attack continues to indulge in fatty foods, the best exercise and stress management program in the world will not save him.

The moderate ways of The Middle Path represent a constructive and sensible philosophy of how to manage one's life in the midst of an intemperate world. When The Middle Path is coupled with the practice of a daily health regimen, the result is an integrated program that can dramatically improve the quality of life.

This theme, that health is dependent on moderation in lifestyle, is both old and new. It is being rediscovered by many modern health experts. In a recent interview, Dr. Dean Ornish, a cardiologist who developed a holistic program for reversing heart disease, emphasized the importance of following a sensible lifestyle:

> *It may seem hard for people to believe that such simple ideas such as sharing feelings or eating a low fat vegetarian diet or doing meditation or walking could have such powerful effects (on disease)....*

In our busy world, we rarely allot time to enjoy the blessings of our relatively short odyssey here on earth. How many of us spend a few moments in quiet introspection or take a moment to say "Thank You"? It is difficult to resist the persistent ringing of the ever-present portable telephone or the urgency of world news breaking from moment to moment. Each new scandal, war, or massacre rivets us to the TV. World events and daily crises pull us away from ourselves and distract us from the real work, that is, the work on ourselves. We will never learn to appreciate the hidden and yet obvious gift of life until we take time to nourish it. We can make time and we can make money, but we can only cultivate sensitivity and a deep awareness for the simple treasures of daily living.

As we approach the end of the twentieth century, popular wisdom does not favor the idea of walking The Middle Path. It is a philosophy that appears out of step, seemingly quaint and slightly archaic. The epoch we live in is one of extremes and conflict in practically all spheres of life. Running in the fast lane is considered the road to success, even though it often leads to broken lives, declining health and dysfunctional relationships. Cutthroat competition is often the name of the game. A deafening din of sight and sound, the electrified tools of powerful media, frequently drowns out the calm voice of reason and the wisdom of a quiet heart. We are witnessing an environmental disaster as The Middle Path is in danger of being paved over by the Information Highway.

We receive most of our health information from without. Every newspaper and national magazine has a health section that informs its readers about the latest medical innovations. The amount of information is overwhelming. But how many of us have stopped for a moment and listened to what our own bodies are telling us? Or listened to the messages from the heart? There is an information highway more relevant to each individual than the internet. It is called the 'innernet.'

Despite living in a difficult age, people long to establish solid families in sane and healthy communities. They want to live full lives where they can enjoy the fruits of their labor; to see their children happy and to play with their grandchildren. The Middle Path offers the means to confront the crucial challenges of our age such as developing healthy personal relationships, improving our physical well-being, and getting to know ourselves better.

The late Rabbi Shlomo Carlebach once said that love begins with the individual and then reaches out to family, community, nation, and the world. He did not mean that we should become narcissistic and selfish. Rather we must learn to love ourselves before we can become giving and whole human beings. This love must translate into an ongoing process of mending our bodies and nourishing our souls. Only then can we be more certain that our contribution will be positive.

This book is about slowing down and enjoying life fully. It is philosophical in tone while providing a moderate and pragmatic way to improve health and to reduce stress. It encourages each individual to make wise choices and to develop healthy habits. There is nothing revolutionary here. There are no promises of 'instant' vitality or 'sure-fire' beauty tips. There is no such thing as a 'moderation' pill. There are no five-year guarantees similar to the promises you get when you buy a car. What's more, unlike a car that works for you, when you follow The Middle Path you have to do the work. This is precisely why this book is so valuable. It is based on the premise that the quality of life will improve from the moment you take off your earphones and listen to your own heart's song.

A Word about "Special Needs"

Throughout this book, I have added a note to modify the exercises for people with 'special needs.' At some time in life, most people will suffer from illness or undergo a medical procedure. Everyone will slow down as a result of growing older. A person with 'special needs' might be receiving chemotherapy as a treatment for cancer or recovering from a bout with hepatitis. Many older people cannot stand on their feet for long periods of time.

In my classes, I try to respond to the different and special needs of each student. When someone complains about the effects of a specific exercise, I try to modify it, so that the student can continue in the class without suffering injury or pain. I've found that the possibilities are limited only by my imagination.

Several years ago, I succeeded in making a breakthrough with regard to 'special needs.' While teaching a class of elderly women in their eighties, I noticed that several of them had sat down while others continued with difficulty. Until then, I had always taught the exercises while standing. Clearly, the way I was teaching was not appropriate to the needs of the class. I asked everyone to sit down for meditation and breathing. During the meditation, I realized that I could do the animal forms (Chapter VIII) while sitting on chairs. After the meditation, I pushed into uncharted territory with the animal forms. The women loved them, particularly the sounds that were linked to a specific animal. Once sitting, they could relax and let themselves go. I learned that most exercises can work if one is willing to be creative.

Sometimes I teach a walking form of meditation called Silk Weaving in which the hands draw the yin/yang symbol in space. For a person in a wheelchair, simply drawing the symbol in space is effective as a meditative exercise. I have another student who was injured in a car accident. After four years, she is still very weak. When she comes to class, she brings a collapsible chair that allows her to rest and remain in the class. She does what she can. I admire her fortitude, and the way many of my students cope with illness and pain.

Everyone is 'differently abled' and that makes them special. Everyone has limits, even the greatest athletes. The Middle Path teaches us that we should respond to who we are and the way we feel. When our legs hurt, particularly knee or ankle pain, we should do the exercises sitting. Avoiding excess and practicing moderation are the keys to a healthy exercise program.

Chapter 1

The Wisdom of the Middle Path

Sometimes breathing is hard and sometimes it comes easily;
Sometimes there is strength and sometimes there is weakness;
Sometimes one is up and sometimes one is down.
Therefore the sage avoids extremes, excesses and complacency.

Lao Tzu in Tao Te Ching

The Growth of Extremism

We are living in a marvelous era. Science and technology have grown more in the last fifty years than they have in the entire previous span of human history. This remarkable leap forward has assumed a life of its own. Spurred on by a natural desire to unravel the mysteries of the universe and to improve the quality of life here on earth, scientists have significantly transformed our lives for the better. We live longer, have grown stronger physically and have access to more knowledge than ever before.

Modern medicine has conquered many diseases that were once deemed incurable. Prostate cancer, for example, now kills only 2 to 3 per cent of those afflicted by it and most live to enjoy a normal life span. A large percentage of those struck by mental illness who until recently might have been hospitalized for an indefinite period, are able to live productive lives through the judicious use of drug therapy. We can fly to distant parts of the world in relative comfort as we watch a movie or listen to the music of our choice. One CD-ROM formatted for easy use contains the knowledge of a 24-volume encyclopedia. It has become a popular cliche to declare that the world has become smaller and that we live in a global village. Never before have the events on one part of the planet so profoundly influenced others who may live thousands of miles away. We could marshal similar evidence to demonstrate that modern people live better qualitatively than our grandparents did or their grandparents before them.

The twentieth century has also witnessed the rise of a powerful belief in the idea of Progress. Many people who live in modern industrial nations and are blessed by fortune and circumstance share this optimistic vision of Progress; namely, that humanity is marching to the beat of a golden age.

Notwithstanding the above evidence, many intelligent people embrace a less optimistic view of Progress. Why is it, they ask, when the future never seemed brighter, dark clouds crowd the horizon? Science is prolonging life as never before and yet people are brutally killing each other on city streets and in ethnic wars all over the world. The knowledge of the ages is spread upon our table, yet many thoughtful people question whether we are any the wiser for it. In the West, people have achieved a relatively high standard of living, and yet a poverty of spiritual and social values pervades and undermines the fabric of these societies. One example is the divorce rate, which in some parts of America is higher than the marriage rate. Another is the flourishing use of illegal drugs that has mushroomed into a major social ill.

There has been a breakdown in social trust and in our ability to communicate with one another. Some social scientists blame the age of television for encouraging the spread of violence. People are spending more time in front of the television and lately the computer instead of enjoying quality time with friends or initiating new social contacts. "Are we forgetting how to talk to one another?" they ask. "Are we unwittingly stepping into a dark cellar of loneliness where virtual reality replaces reality itself?" One recent study showed that people who spend an hour or more each day on the internet are generally more lonely and depressed than those who do not. This conclusion surprised the researchers who anticipated that the internet would stimulate social contacts.

In the United States the crime rate is soaring and undergoing a disquieting transformation. Recently *The International Herald Tribune* reported: "The proportion of people slain by family members has sharply declined while the number killed in robberies and by strangers has grown in the 1990s." The reason for this shift in statistics, according to prosecutors and criminologists, is the spread of firearms, the drug trade, and a growing number of violent juvenile offenders. What is frightening about this American phenomenon is that when killing becomes random and senseless, people begin to feel insecure in their communities. There is a logic to crimes of passion and a sense of safety surrounding them that, in most cases, insulates the innocent bystander from them. But random violence is something we can do little to control and seems closer to the gambler whose fate hangs on the turn of the roulette wheel. To paraphrase Albert Einstein, we want to believe that God does not play dice with the universe, or with our lives. When violence seems to be the improvisation of chance, it creates a pervading sense of insecurity that breeds extremist responses. People arm themselves. Trust becomes a luxury of the foolhardy.

The Economic Roots of Societal Dis-ease

In recent years, insecurity born of economic and social frustration has grown in most Western countries. Young people share the same values that their parents did twenty-five years ago. They want to own their own homes, to have well-paying positions with job security, and to raise their children in a healthy, safe environment. Yet for many, this American dream has become only a mirage on the distant horizon. In the 1990s young people have to work harder for less monetary compensation than their parents did. Studies have shown that while productivity of the American workers is growing, they are working longer hours in order to maintain their buying power. Until recently, one salary was enough to meet the needs of a middle-class family. This is no longer true. For most families, it takes two salaries. The economic picture can be distressingly bleak for single parents. In addition, advances in technology and foreign job competition have combined to increase the general sense of job insecurity. Today, being a doctor, a dentist, or a lawyer is not the sure road to prosperity that it was in the past.

Many people are caught in a vise-like, no-win situation. They must push themselves in order to stay competitive and relatively job secure. On the other hand, a 1991 *Time*-CNN survey reported that 69% of those surveyed would like to "slow down and live a more relaxed life." Only 19% wanted to increase their pace of life. 61% felt that their jobs require so much effort that as one person reported, "it's difficult to find time to enjoy life". A large majority wanted to spend more time with their families. These kinds of chronic tensions are a major cause of many illnesses from ulcers to severe depression.

There is another side to this problem. In a society that places a premium on consumerism, the business-oriented media encourage people to want more and to want it now. Yet, for the middle class, the relatively well-off no less than the poor, the gloom of scarcity marks their daily lives: "the day late and dollar short syndrome." Many find themselves only treading water, struggling to pay off their credit card debts. "I'm just surviving," explained the father of one middle-income family in Time magazine, "I'm not succeeding." Unless one is extremely wealthy, no matter what one has, it does not seem to be enough. How can this be?

One way of analyzing this paradox is by looking through the lens of "wants" and "needs." There is a direct relationship between the quickening tempo of technology and the burgeoning growth of what people want. The array of goods and services from the personal computer to the high cost of college tuition puts today's middle income earners behind the economic eight ball in a way that their parents did not encounter. The dilemma we face is that the horizons and costs of technology appear to be infinite, human desires are infinite, while people suffer psychologically, emotionally, and physically from the strictures of human limitations. This is the rub. We are limited by the fact that we die, by the amount of time we have to expend on things, by the endurance of our bodies, and by our incomes. The luck of the draw also curtails the dreams of who we could be. Circumstance and natural talent exert a powerful influence on what we can and cannot achieve.

Yet, driven to be as beautiful as a Hollywood movie star, as successful as a wealthy businessman or as popular as an elected politician, many people ride out to realize the impossible dream. Like Don Quixote who has read too many chivalrous stories on romance, we devour the most recent self-help bestseller that promises to reveal how to become all things that we are not. The implicit message of these books and the advertising media is that there is something wrong with us. If only we would buy their product, we could be more attractive, thinner, happier, stronger, richer, and, finally, more successful in everything we choose to do. Yet how many people on the heavy side of "perfect" have suffered feelings of inferiority, spent countless hours of worry, and doled out untold dollars of their hard-earned wages in search of the "ideal" weight?

The disease of discontentment knows no limits and plays no favorites. It afflicts the rich as well as the poor, the white-collar as well as the blue-collar worker. Lao Tzu, the great Chinese sage, captured the tragic consequences of untamed desires with these wise words:

> *There is no calamity greater than lavish desires,*
> *There is no greater guilt than discontentment,*
> *And there is no greater disaster than greed.*
> *He who is contented with contentment is always contented.*

When desires born out of feelings of insecurity are fanned indiscriminately, they transform normal human aspirations into insatiable ambitions. One loses the sense of self and center. Something external – the things we possess and the way others view us – defines who we are. Unwittingly we exchange the role of being masters of our destiny for being slaves to our senses. Lao Tzu warned against adopting the slave mentality, observing: "the wise man is guided by what he feels and not by what he sees." In order to make intelligent decisions, individuals must tune in to their internal compass and allow it to serve as a knowing and intimate guide to who they are and what they truly need.

Wants and Needs

The refrain of a famous Rolling Stones song goes like this: "You can't always get what you want, but if you try sometimes you just might get what you need." The apparent contradiction between enjoying a relatively high standard of living and suffering never-ending scarcity turns on what set of lifestyle priorities one chooses. This decision-making process reflects the way in which one views "wants" and "needs." What is the difference between them?

"Needs" are those tangible and intangible things or aspirations that are absolutely essential for us to survive and flourish. We need food to maintain our health and love to give us a sense of emotional fulfillment. We would die without the one and we cannot live fully without the other. "Wants," on the other hand, are desires that demand immediate psychological gratification. "Wants" arise out of ego compulsion or some momentary fascination. The person consumed by "wants" is like a child who begs for a particular toy, plays with it for a moment and then throws it away. Without pausing, he is off chasing his next object of desire. For most of us, a "need" is a reliable car that comfortably gets us to where we wish to go. A "want" is desiring to possess a stable of luxury cars, some of which you may only drive once a year, if ever. An example of a "need" is a person who eats in order to live. An example of a "want" is a glutton who lives in order to eat.

The above song of the Rolling Stones makes a clear distinction between "wants" and "needs" and points to the wisdom of sticking to basics. Only by understanding the difference between the two can we begin to strip away the unessential from the essential, that which pays homage only to our egos and that which serves our real needs. Eventually, through a process of maturation, an adult realizes that lasting happiness and satisfaction will not come in orgies of instant gratification. Indeed learning to brake the powerful urges for compulsive gratification is a key component in enjoying life moment to moment, completely, and with a deepening sense of staying in touch with reality.

We can greatly reduce the pressures of modern living by focusing on "needs" rather than "wants." By limiting an obsession with material goods or fleeting pleasures and by focusing on one's "natural" experience, life evolves to a simpler, more enjoyable, and less pretentious way of being in the world. Similar to the sculptor who chips away everything not needed, we must carefully chip away the extraneous components of our lifestyle. In simplifying, however, we need not become simpleminded. One travels lightly yet with feet firmly rooted in the ground and a mind untethered to an overabundance of material comforts or the seductions of momentary pleasures. One is free to explore the wonders of the universe and not be overly dazzled by wonderment. We gradually come to accept ourselves as we are and not as a distorted reflection of what others expect us to be. We become "normal" human beings because we settle into the shapes and patterns of our natural selves. We become "grounded" in who we are and what we need.

I have a friend who was living a life of sensual delight that many would envy. Yet he confided to me that he was very lonely and unfulfilled. He wanted to marry, settle down and have children. He complained that he couldn't find that "right" someone. Suddenly, it came to him that he must become celibate. He did this for three years and then met his future wife. He now has a happy marriage and children. The problem with my friend was that he was so overwhelmed with wants that he couldn't find the one he needed. In his case, celibacy trimmed his wings and brought him down to earth.

By the same token, we need not follow the path of the Buddha, give away our worldly goods and become ascetics in order to know ourselves. We need not become celibate like my friend. We can become the real thing by being absolutely clear as to our genuine needs in all aspects of our lives and then by negotiating a meaningful path between the extremes of excess and insufficiency. In his classic book, *Small is Beautiful*, E. F. Schumacher speaks of the economic Middle Path for nations that equally applies to individuals: "It is a question of finding the right path of development, the Middle Way, between materialist heedlessness and traditional immobility...." This path is not found only in the solitude of a mountain cabin or along the lonely shores of the sea but each moment "it is close to you, in your mouth and in your heart." Wherever you are, that is where it is. Each of us in our own way within ourselves can walk The Middle Path of wellness and well-being.

Foundations of The Middle Path

Historically, there were advocates of The Middle Path in almost all traditional societies. In a world where religious values informed the ambiance of day to day interactions, sages and prophets taught their fellow human beings how best to live their lives. They wrote, exhorted, and served as examples in order to light the way to a "virtuous" life. Their teachings benefited the individual as well as society. In a community that emphasized the virtue of honesty, for example, there was likely to be a prevailing condition of social harmony in personal and business relationships. In contrast, a society that strayed too far or too fast from its moral foundations was likely to suffer social and economic strife.

While the above example of honesty indicated a positive good, it was also an abstract principle that could be difficult to put into practice. Too much honesty can be destructive. When taken to extremes, honesty often smacks of arrogance and self-righteousness. The Middle Path posed one way in which an abstract principle such as honesty might be judiciously and wisely employed. It allowed the individual to avoid the dangerous pitfalls of extremism. The Middle Path served as a counterweight to immoderate outbursts of moral posturing because it counseled a way of balance, temperance, and circumspection. As a philosophy of moderation, it provided an inherent system of checks and balances on fanaticism while rejecting the notion that the end justifies the means.

In Western culture the Bible is an excellent source for The Middle Path, often lauding the virtues of steering a moderate course:

> *Do not be too righteous or too wise,*
> *Why isolate yourself (from the world)?* (Ecclesiasties 7:16)

and
> *Walk a balanced path*
> *And make all your ways firm.*
> *Do not turn to the right or the left,*
> *And you will remove yourself from harm.* (Proverbs 4:26)

One of my favorite Biblical passages describing The Middle Path is also found in Proverbs:
> *Remove far from me vanity and lies:*
> *Give me neither poverty or riches;*
> *Feed me with my allotted portion:*
> *Lest I become sated and deny you,*
> *And say, Who is the Lord?*
> *Or lest I be poor, and steal,*
> *And violate the name of my God.* (Proverbs 30:8-10)

Unlike its Western counterpart, Chinese culture evolved without the moral imperatives of a Divine Being. The principles of balance and harmony based on

Nature's moral laws underpinned the Chinese worldview. This philosophy easily lent itself to the notion of The Middle Path. Confucius, the most influential Chinese teacher, often praised the virtues of following The Middle Path.

> Tzu-Kung asked, 'who was the better man, Shih or Shang?'
> Confucius said, 'Shih goes too far and Shang does not go far enough.'
> Tzu-Kung said, 'then Shih is better?'
> Confucius said, 'to go too far is the same as not to go far enough.'

Or

> Confucius said, '(Emperor) Shun was a man of great wisdom!
> He loved to question others and to examine their words, however ordinary.
> He concealed what was bad in them and displayed what was good.
> He took hold of their two extremes, took the mean between them
> And applied it in his dealings with the people.
> This was how he became Shun (the sage-emperor).'

Confucius also advocated moderation in the way one conducts his or her life. He believed that by walking The Middle Path one can live wisely, contribute to the betterment of society, and not be overwhelmed by superfluous distractions. He summed up the way of moderation as the following:

> I know why the Way (of harmony between man and nature) is not pursued.
> The intelligent go beyond it and the unintelligent do not reach it.
> I know why the Way is not understood.
> The worthy go beyond it and the unworthy do not reach it.
> Everyone eats and drinks, but few really taste the flavor.

According to Confucius, hitting the mark is not a matter of intelligence or worthiness, although both are needed. More important is the virtue of balance and sensitivity. When he speaks of taste, he is emphasizing the distinction between quality and quantity. Tasting the flavor requires one to slow down, concentrate, and go to the heart of the matter. How many of us really taste the food in a fast-food restaurant? How many of us stuff ourselves at a meal and feel full, yet unsatisfied? How many of us sleep eight hours and awake exhausted? How many of us make love and feel empty?

When we use the word "make" in the context of love, it suggests that love is a product that is quantifiable. But who can measure love's depths and who can define its boundaries?

In Buddhism The Middle Path played such an important role that all schools claimed to teach its virtues, although they differed in interpretation. The Middle Path or Way represented an attempt by Buddhists to synthesize two opposing or extreme philosophical positions such as the contradictory notions of Absolute and Relative truth. This tendency to harmonize extremes carried over into Buddhist societies as a whole. The idea of being mindful, that is to say, being consciously aware in everyday life, meant a slowing down of the pace and confronting reality in an honest, no-nonsense way. From the Buddhist perspective, extreme thoughts or actions were exceptions rather than the rule.

In Chinese Taoism, The Middle Path also found a strong advocacy in the notion of Wu Wei. Wu Wei is often translated as "no action." It actually means no "unnatural" action that opposes the way in which the universe functions (Tao). To be in accord with Wu Wei, one must act spontaneously and harmoniously with the needs of the present moment while eschewing activity that is excessively strenuous or strained. The best analogy for Wu Wei is water. In the environment water flows naturally toward an incline, following the path of least resistance. Similarly, when a person follows The Middle Path, he or she must know when to change direction, to bend with the needs of the moment, and yet to stay on course. The Middle Path is a strategy for being successful in achieving one's goals despite temporary setbacks, detours, or delays.

The Middle Path is not limited to the realm of virtue or morality nor is it only an abstract principle. Rather it is a way of being in the world, a supple response to ever changing circumstances. It is neither "this nor that," as the Chinese sage Chuang Tzu was fond of saying, but holding to the center. The person sees all the possibilities from the wisdom of perspective.

Physical and Mental Health according to *The Middle Path*

First and foremost, The Middle Path is a practical way to further one's wellness and well-being that spills over into all spheres of daily life. Most cultures clearly perceived a direct correlation between a judicious and moderate choice of lifestyle and the ability to maintain good health. "Choice" meant that the mind was actively involved in making the appropriate decisions for the way a person conducted his or her life. If either mind or body was subjected to the extreme pressures of stress for extended periods of time, disease was likely to follow. Hence, "wisdom" literature of the past often spoke of The Middle Path as the best method to ensure a healthy body and mind.

Traditional cultures were also profoundly aware that the wellness of the body and the well-being of the mind could not be separated. In the Talmud, the Rabbis taught:"...cleanliness leads to restraint, restraint leads to purity, (and) purity leads to holiness..."(Avoda Zarah 20b). They understood that physical purity was a prerequisite for spiritual purity. In fact, Jews were forbidden to live in a town that did not have a physician or public bath. In this context, the cliche "cleanliness is next to godliness" assumes its original profound meaning.

Hippocrates (460-370 BCE), the father of Western medicine whose influence extended as far afield as India and Tibet, was a strong advocate of The Middle Path. He believed that disease was caused by imbalances within and without the body. Historically, he is one of the earliest known advocates of preventive medicine. Hippocrates taught that the physician should fortify the sick patient with a healthy diet and proper hygiene. Any kind of extreme or invasive treatment should be left as a last resort. On the whole, he also opposed any drastic changes in one's health habits:

> *It is dangerous to disturb the body violently*
> *whether it be by starvation or by feeding,*
> *by making it hot or cold, or in any way whatsoever.*
> *All excesses are inimical to nature.*
> *It is safe to proceed a little at a time,*
> *especially when changing from one regimen to another.*

Moses Maimonides

Moses Maimonides, the great Jewish rabbi, philosopher and physician (1135-1204), was a disciple of the Hippocratic tradition. He advocated the use of preventive medicine and the use of herbs as cures for disease. So famous were his healing talents that he became the personal physician to the Sultan of Egypt along with ministering to a huge private practice. His interest in preventive medicine and religious philosophy led Maimonides to advocate a way of body/mind health, which he called "The Middle Path". In one of the clearest and most comprehensive explanations of The Middle Path, he defined his concept thus:

The right way is the intermediate quality of every disposition of man, and that is the disposition which is equidistant from both extremes, being neither nearer to the one nor to the other. The ancient sages have therefore commanded that a man should always put, arrange, and direct his dispositions in the middle course, so that he may be sound in his body....This way is the way of the wise.

Maimonides described the personalities of human beings as leaning toward one extreme or another. There were many possibilities. One person might incline toward anger while another toward meekness, one toward avarice while another toward asceticism. According to Maimonides who was a man of logic and great spiritual will, each person should evaluate the nature of his or her personality, discover its tendencies and then direct it along The Middle Path. The Middle Path lay at some intermediate point from either extremes of his or her personality. A person should not be easily angered nor, as Maimonides put it, "be like one who is dead and without feeling...(rather) he should express anger only over an important thing...in order to prevent it from happening again." He explained that sometimes a parent must show outwardly that he is angry with a child to emphasize a point, yet internally must remain calm and clearheaded. True to the supple approach of The

Middle Path, Maimonides does not rule out controlled anger as a method to effect a positive result.

Maimonides emphasized that maintaining good health was a vital component in serving God. In doing so, the cultivation of a healthy body ascended to its apotheosis and became a religious imperative:

> *Since maintaining a healthy and sound body is among the ways of God –*
> *for one cannot understand or have any knowledge of the creator, if*
> *he is ill – therefore, he must avoid that which harms the body and accustom*
> *himself to that which is healthful and helps the body to become stronger.*

If Maimonides' words seem a bit on the strong side, think of a time when you were sick with the flu. You probably found it difficult to watch television or read a book, let alone trying to serve God. To his way of thinking, serving God was an active and constant endeavor, physically and mentally. Anything that inhibited this comprehensive service prevented one from reaching his or her full potential. Thus, as a doctor, he counseled his patients and followers to practice The Middle Path, spiritually as well as physically, in order to stay healthy.

What is particularly significant in Maimonides' thought is the link between a person's emotional disposition and the health of the body. Maimonides' Middle Path carried over into all areas of life including diet and charity. He recommended that people should keep regular hours and eat only when hungry. He also believed strongly in the efficacy of temperate exercise.

Closer to our own time, Abraham Lincoln represented the epitome of the way in which one travels The Middle Path. He was known for his calm and compassionate demeanor. He spent a good part of the day meeting with many of those who came to the White House, from the highest echelons to the downtrodden, from favor-seekers to those with tales of woe. He lifted the downhearted and counseled those in distress. He treated everyone with concern and respect. During the Civil War, he practiced the virtue of forgiveness and often pardoned young soldiers who had deserted, an offense that carried the death penalty. In a time of inflamed political passions, he had the uncommon ability to listen calmly to another's hot-tempered point of view and then press his own views to the forefront.

At first impression the mild-mannered president seemed like an easy mark, a hick from the sticks, a piece of putty to be shaped by the will of others who were more sophisticated than he. Yet Lincoln's personality was soft as cotton on the outside and tempered steel on the inside. "So deft had been Lincoln's leadership," writes his biographer Benjamin P. Thomas, "that people often failed to recognize it. Few persons thought him great. His strength was flexible, like fine-spun wire, sensitive to every need and pressure, yielding but never breaking. Forced to adopt hard measures, he had tempered them with clemency. He exercised stern powers leniently, with regard for personal feelings and respect for human rights."

From this description, Lincoln appears to encapsulate Lao Tzu's counsel: "'Yield and overcome; bend and be straight."

One better understands Lincoln's wisdom in this advice that he imparted to his son concerning the dangers of anger:

> *Quarrel not at all. No man resolved to make the most of himself, can spare the time for personal contention. Still less can he afford to take all the consequences, including the vitiating of his temper, and the loss of self-control.*

But controlling anger is only the first step. The second, practicing forgiveness, allows people to be compassionate and to love one another. Forgiveness offers the opportunity to wipe out animosity and to walk the road of reconciliation. The ultimate paradigm for forgiveness rests in the character of the Almighty. As God passes by him, Moses affirms his Master's compassion: "The Lord, The Lord, mighty, merciful and gracious, long-suffering and abundant in love and truth, keeping kindness to the thousandth generation, forgiving iniquity, transgression and sin...." Jews are reminded of these traits during holidays and particularly on the Day of Atonement. If Jews are to be forgiven by God, they must first forgive one another.

In Christianity, Jesus expressed great strength of character when he asked forgiveness for those who tormented him. One wonders what the world would be like if all of humanity sought to live this ideal.

The Middle Path is a philosophy that shows the way to a healthy body and mind. Its essence rejects extremes and excesses of every kind. Its source is rooted solidly in the universal wisdom of the past; a moving spirit that transverses borders, cultures, and national character. It is neither East nor West, Christian nor Buddhist, Jewish nor Islamic. The Middle Path is not an ideology but rather a common-sense, no-nonsense way of thinking. It provides us with an overview of how to live more sensibly and to get more enjoyment from life. The Middle Path is a philosophy of wholeness.

Diet and The Middle Path

One of the most important aspects of health is diet and dieting. This topic elicits intense public interest. If you browse the health section of your local bookstore, you will find that it is liberally supplied with books on practically every imaginable kind of diet notion. Many of these diets emphasize a unique approach such as the all-pasta diet to lose weight, the meatless protein diet, or the macrobiotic diet where food is mixed and cooked according to the oriental principles of Yin and Yang.

In contrast, The Middle Path does not advise you what to eat and what not to eat. Rather it is a way of being sensible and moderate in the general way you conduct your life. By suggesting that you avoid extremes, The Middle Path focuses on your individual health needs. If you decide to change your normal diet, do it gradually, with careful thought, and under the guidance of someone with professional qualifications in the field of nutrition.

At the same time, there is much that you can do on your own. Pay attention to what foods agree with you and what foods do not. If, for example, wine or chocolate give you a headache, this is a good sign that this drink or food is not one in which you should indulge. If you are overweight to the point where your blood pressure is high, you should begin a moderate diet to lower your weight and thus protect your overall health. Crash diets are beyond the pale of The Middle Path. In fact recent studies show that 90% of the people who in a short time dramatically reduce their weight, within two years are back to where they started. Sensible weight control is a matter of lifestyle, not fads or fashion. Similarly, I often remind my students that the benefits from The Middle Path accrue over the long run and are cumulative. Beware of the quick fix.

The diet of The Middle Path should be determined by age, the seasons of the year, the person's constitution and the habits of one's social environment. It can be risky to deviate too much from the diet you grew up with, unless it clearly crosses the boundary of what is known to be scientifically healthy. A better approach is to modify your diet in order to conform with objective standards of health and your personal requirements. Most importantly, do it gradually, as Hippocrates advised, a little at a time. In winter most people need to eat heavier foods like meat or hot cereals while in summer a diet of lighter foods such as fruit and salads are appropriate.

You should not eat quickly but rather take time to chew. A pleasant unhurried environment creates an ambiance where the stomach has time to properly digest and absorb the meal. Regular eating habits and the size of the portions are also crucial. For many people, regular meals, often three times a day, are necessary for them to function normally.

Maimonides recommended that a person should eat only when he is hungry and drink only when he is thirsty. His thoughts echo the way in which the Buddhist Po-Chang described the essence of Zen: "When I am hungry, I eat; when I am thirsty, I drink." As a physician, Maimonides believed that the two greatest sins that vitiated good health were not relieving oneself immediately on sensing the need and immoderate eating habits. "Overeating," he averred, "is like poison to the body." He stated that this is true even if one eats healthy foods. In this vein Maimonides wrote:

> *A person should not eat until his stomach is full.*
> *Rather, he should stop eating when he has eaten*
> *close to three quarters full in satisfaction.*

The above advice of Maimonides is invaluable to someone seeking a healthy diet and wishing to lose weight. It was pointed out that losing weight and keeping it off has more to do with a lifestyle of dietary moderation than with the particular foods one eats. However, there are foods that are unhealthy even when taken in moderation. The biggest problem with fattening desserts, for example, is not the calories but rather the fact that they can be addictive both physically and psychologically. Once you begin eating fudge sundaes, your taste buds will crave more.

Cheng Man Ch'ing, the Chinese physician and T'ai Chi master, held that moderation in all aspects of one's life was the key to good health. Like Maimonides, he recommended that people should not overeat. They should leave the table a little hungry. Being blessed with an inventive mind, Professor Ch'ing elaborated on the idea of moderation by using the example of extremes:

> *There is no poison that cannot aid health in the right circumstance*
> *And no 'virtuous substance' that will not be poisonous in excess.*

Benjamin Franklin, who in 1790 died at the ripe old age of 84, was also a practitioner of The Middle Path. In the colonies before Independence he became famous for his wit and commonsense philosophy as expressed in Poor Richard's Almanack. "Eat and drink such an exact Quantity," he wrote,

> *"as the constitution*
> *of thy body allows of,*
> *in reference to Services of the mind.*
> *They that study much,*
> *ought not to eat so much as those that work hard,*
> *their digestion being not so good.*
> <u>*Excess in all other things,*</u>
> <u>*as well as in Meat and Drink,*</u>
> <u>*is also to be avoided.*</u> (my emphasis)

As an advocate of The Middle Path, Ben Franklin also proposed his own Golden Rule for generally making the best of life:

> *Be studious in your profession, and you will be learned.*
> *Be industrious and frugal, and you will be rich.*
> *Be sober and temperate, and you will be healthy.*
> *Be in general virtuous, and you will be happy.*
> *At least you will, by such conduct, stand the best chance*
> *for such consequences.*

Exercise and The Middle Path

Recently a friend died while jogging. A jogger for thirty years, he was running and collapsed from an apparent heart attack. There are a few very good reasons why he should not have been jogging that day. First of all, he had a family history of heart problems. Although he had no known heart problems, his father had died of a heart attack some twenty-five years before while exercising. Another reason is that he chose to jog during the heat of a summer's day. Finally, he was just getting back into shape after a six-month hiatus due to a leg injury. He was probably not as fit as he thought.

Exercise is absolutely essential in order to maintain a healthy body! No one disputes this. But what kind of exercise and for whom? Similar to our above discussion of diet, each individual should choose his or her regimen of exercise based on age, the seasons of the year, a person's constitution, and social/physical environment. The goal of The Middle Path is to maximize the benefits and to minimize the risks.

Maimonides believed that exercise was invaluable in preserving good health:

As long as one exercises, exerts himself greatly,
does not eat to the point of satiation and has loose bowels,
he will not suffer sickness and he will grow in strength.
This applies even if he eats harmful foods.

The person who follows The Middle Path can jog if he or she wishes. But that person should be aware that the aging body can no longer endure the same physical stress that it could when it was younger. This is a hard lesson to accept and learn. It is a fact of life that many people wish to ignore, often with disastrous consequences. One reason for this arises out of the mythology of the "baby boom" generation, who are now fifty and long to remain "forever young."

One of my T'ai Chi teachers, Benjamin Pang Jeng Lo, spoke about the aging process when he was in his late sixties. Most of us in the class were much younger than he, yet not one of us could match his exceptional strength and vitality. He said that after forty years of age, the body begins to decline in its physical prowess. What T'ai Chi can do for a person, he explained, is to slow down that process of deterioration because it strengthens and conserves the body's energy. This is the wisdom of The Middle Path, the conservation of one's energy. A spendthrift with his energy will soon find himself broken just as a fool will be soon departed of his money. On the other hand, through the wisdom of experience and moderation, it is possible, with a little bit of luck, to enjoy an "indian summer" of vitality in the winter years.

T'ai Chi is but one kind of exercise that conforms with the ideas of The Middle Path. There are many others such as swimming, bicycle riding, walking, and even jogging. Because The Middle Path is an attitude rather than a formal regimen, almost any exercise can be adapted to its philosophy. Remember, The Middle Path is a way of being, not a dogmatic ideology. It is not a program with steadfast rules of engagement. If one is older than forty and wishes to jog, he or she should be careful as to how long, how fast, and the time of day. At some point later in life, the jogger may wish to exchange his running shoes for walking or hiking boots.

The seasons of the year should influence what type of sport we choose to do. Most people enjoy swimming and water skiing in the summer and snow skiing and ice skating in the winter. It makes good sense not to overdo an exercise like jogging in the summer or to swim out of doors in winter. Hippocrates put it this way:

Those who enjoy gymnastics should run and wrestle during the winter;
in summer wrestling should be restricted and running forbidden,
but long walks in the cool part of the day should take their place.

You should also take care not to overemphasize competition with yourself or with others. For the young, competition is healthy and contains little risk. The body is strong and can be pushed to great heights. Most bodies of thirty-five and younger can take and even thrive on the ardor of intense competition. After thirty-five to forty, there is a clear process of deterioration. We can see this with professional athletes who are rarely able to continue at the zenith of their sport after thirty-five.

For the ordinary athlete, the aging process is less clearly defined because he or she usually does not push as hard as the professional athlete. Nonetheless, it is happening to everybody. The danger of intense athletic competition in later life is that one watches only the clock for the best time instead of taking time to be aware of nature's clock.

According to the way of The Middle Path, you must know yourself and your body in order to make intelligent decisions as to what you can and cannot do. On the deepest levels, The Middle Path is not only about making decisions based on reasoned judgment. It also honors intuition. You must listen to the needs of your body and the whispers of your heart. To do that, you must nurture the stillness of contemplation within your movement.

The way of The Middle Path is to seek a modality of balance and harmony between who we are, where we are in the context of our physical condition, and what type of exercise we choose to do. Ideally, we should strive to instill the philosophy of moderation into our way of being until its outlook becomes second nature, so that it becomes as natural as our mother tongue.

Summary

The Middle Path does not herald a program of action of its own. It is not an ideology with specific goals or agendas. Rather it is an intuition leading toward a particular lifestyle, a way of being, and a mode of thinking. The Middle Path is a guide to help us perceive reality as it is and thus to live more genuine and fulfilling lives. Once grasped, it becomes the moving spirit that sets the tone and renders the ambiance for every imaginable human activity.

The Middle Path does not demand parallel thought patterns or actions from its adherents. Two people could practice two different kinds of diet, for example, and still be on The Middle Path. The Middle Path recognizes that each person is unique and, as such, has individual needs.

The Middle Path is forged on a trail of ordinary miracles and framed by the poignancy of the moment. It proclaims that every "now" is forever. Too often we are wowed by astounding acts of magic, seductive airs of mystery, or the powerful exercise of authority. In contrast, The Middle Path is composed of everyday events so commonplace that we forget how miraculous they are. A few that come to mind are the fact that we are alive and able to partake in the wonders of the world, that we can love and be loved, and that we can exercise some control over our destiny. These simple miracles are not hidden in a puff of smoke or in the bedazzlement of illusion. They occur at every moment and wherever one goes. They are miracles of the heart.

The basic premises of The Middle Path are to know oneself, to avoid extremes and to exercise a sensible intelligence with an open mind in all matters. The impulse that leads to The Middle Path is twofold: it emerges out of the quiet depths of one's inner being and is informed by the collective human experience. As such, it combines knowledge and intuition to produce a unique personal persuasion. By virtue of its genuineness, those on The Middle Path exude the qualities of strength, wisdom, and self-confidence. And yet, to the veteran of this path, there is nothing special about the journey because it is simply an authentic reflection of being oneself.

Practical Exercise:

A Change of Mind

You have, I hope, been moved to change some aspects of your life by bringing your lifestyle in accord with The Middle Path. So how do you go about it?

I believe that the first step is to understand the power of the mind and its relationship to the world we live in. Your mind is the first cause that starts the ball rolling. It is the key to change. This may be the most important idea you will learn from this book.

The following is the Law for Transformation: **Consciousness > Energy > Material World.** Consciousness produces and directs Energy, and Energy effects change in the Material World. In martial arts, we understand this formula in the following way: the mind directs the energy and then the energy called Ch'i manifests itself through movement in and by the body. When you see martial artists breaking bricks with their hands, they are demonstrating this principle. They focus their mind before the break, bring their Ch'i to their hands, and then they break the brick. The proper focus and the energy are the keys, not the power of the muscles. The outer structure is secondary to the power of the mind.

According to the Law of Transformation, if you want to change the physical world, you must first change yourself. You must change the way you think, which means that you must change your consciousness.

But you can't sit around all day, thinking wonderful thoughts and expecting the material world to change. This is a form of delusion. You must also act in the material world. There must be a dialectical relationship between your changes of consciousness and your actions in daily life. You must be a thinker and a doer. The one reinforces the other. The person who breaks bricks has put in a tremendous amount of physical and mental preparation, perhaps years, before he or she is ready.

In Jewish tradition, there is a saying of the Rabbis: "Don't expect to gain anything without exerting effort."

Take, for example, an individual who wants to be a competitive weightlifter. If he only imagines lifting at his peak performance and never touches the barbell, he is certain to do poorly. On the other hand, studies on athletes in various sports demonstrate conclusively that visualization in combination with physical training is the optimal approach to attain peak performances. This is one important way in which the mind exercises the body.

The mind and the body are entwined in a marvelous dialectical, an interplay and an encounter, that is both sublime and mysterious. To say they are one is true but is also an oversimplification. Each has its unique functions that, like a marriage, combine to create something more than its parts.

So what does this have to do with walking The Middle Path? By making incremental changes in our consciousness while taking steps to live in a sensible way, we can initiate and institute positive transformations in our lives that resonate with the wisdom of The Middle Path. We become healthier and more conscious human beings. Our conscience becomes more fully developed and can speak out powerfully for what we believe is right and what is wrong. Our dreams of who we want to be begin to materialize and come true.

The other day I was driving home after a busy day. I was tired. All I wanted to do was to read a good book and listen to music. I also have a wife and young children waiting for me at home. My wife had been with the kids all afternoon and I knew she was also tired. As I drove home, I decided to focus on my family's needs instead of mine at that particular moment. I decided that I would put the kids to bed and read them a story. I also decided that I would clean up the supper dishes. These decisions represented a change in my consciousness, a change in the direction of my energy, and, as it turned out, a positive change in what happened that evening. I did get to read and listen to music but it was much later than I had first planned. My children were delighted that I spent time with them and my wife was grateful for the help. The change in my attitude helped to create an entirely different and positive family dynamic than if I had returned home grumpy and resentful of their demands. It was the laws of transformation in action.

This is how the following meditation works. It is easy to do. You only have to choose one of the topics below that are relevant to your day and meditate on it. For example, how could you do something better? Let's say that you overate at lunch. Think about how it made you feel. Bloated? Uncomfortable? Fat? Direct your consciousness to eat less at your next meal. As Maimonides recommended, leave the table a little hungry. In the larger picture, you might want to focus on a problem of insatiable "wants." Often a specific problem (overeating) reflects a broader issue (insatiable wants and a lack of control).

Each evening, think about your day and decide which step of The Middle Path you need to work on. When I do this exercise, I imagine an encounter that I could have handled better. I've listed fourteen ways to improve your interaction with the world. I'm sure that you could think of some others that are more relevant to your life. The key to change lies first and foremost with your consciousness. But remember, you must also do. This exercise requires the "doing"'

Review the following list. Close your eyes and think about your day. Focus on something in it that you would like to change using one of the following suggestions. Keep it simple. Don't try to do more than one thing.

1. Reconnect with your unique inner vision through meditation and contemplation, know yourself.
2. Strive to become more honest and open, fostering a sense of personal integrity.
3. Develop a calm and balanced temperament in daily life.
4. Control anger.
5. Be ready to admit mistakes.
6. Practice forgiveness.
7. Learn and practice various meditation exercises to regulate stress.
8. Exercise the body daily.

9. Slow down and relax.
10. Make time for recreation.
11. Switch to a healthy diet.
12. Eat slowly.
13. Do not overeat.
14. Love someone or something.

Chapter 2

A Warm-up for the Middle Path

*Our bodies were designed to move,
and they can't stay healthy if we spend
all our time sitting or lying down.
People who exercise regularly
have fewer illnesses than sedentary persons.*
Dr. Bernie S. Siegel, M.D. in *Love, Medicine & Miracles*

Introduction

In Jerusalem where I live, there is a woman who is seventy-eight years old and still teaching ballet. Her name is Klara Landau Bondy. A vibrant and active woman, she recently confided her secret of staying healthy: "Your body is something you need to oil. If you don't oil it, one day it will break." She "oils" her body through dance.

Using similar imagery, the Chinese have a saying: "The body is like a door hinge: If you don't oil it through movement, it will become rusty." The Chinese also compare our bodies to a pool of water. If the water becomes stagnant, it will soon become polluted and a breeding place for disease.

Everyone agrees that the body needs exercise in order to thrive and to preserve itself. Disagreements arise over how much and what kind of exercise. The commonsense approach of The Middle Path advises that the correct choice of exercise should depend on the age of the person, the physical condition of the body and the person's temperament. All three are equally important.

Unfortunately many people choose a form of exercise that they do not enjoy. They often employ the wrong criteria and select an exercise that conforms to the fad of the day. This is something like choosing a mate on the basis of beauty or economic considerations alone. It helps to have a successful and lasting relationship if you love the person. The same is true for whatever regimen you choose. To miss a day would leave you incomplete.

I have an uncle who is ninety-eight years old and still in excellent health. Recently he told me that his immediate goal is to live two more years. If so, he says, he will have lived in three centuries. For the last seventy years, give or take a few years, he begins the morning with a moderate set of strengthening and stretching exercises. He still swims.

Physical limitations are also important factors in considering an appropriate exercise program. For example, I once enjoyed jogging and playing basketball. A knee operation some years ago precluded the rigors of running and jumping as a viable option for me. The surgeon advised me that, because of jogging's high impact on the body, over time I would probably re-injure my knee. As an alternative, I ride an exercise bike in my living room along with doing a few low-impact aerobic exercises.

This style of workout suits my particular inclinations, age and physical condition. While Chinese health exercises remain the central features of my exercise program, in order to stay healthy an appropriate amount of aerobic work is absolutely necessary, particularly to reduce weight. Recently the *International Herald Tribune* reported: "Inactivity has a major deleterious influence on the weight of Americans...Only about one American in five gets enough exercise to keep weight down and health up. And there is virtually no exercise in the lives of sixty percent of Americans." Anyone who wishes to stay healthy cannot afford to be on the downside of those statistics. In the vast field of exercise there is a staggering array of methods and techniques from which to choose. With a little effort and research most people will find a program that is suitable to their needs.

What's different about this Warm-up?

The exercises in this chapter share a common thread of "strenuous moderation" with my uncle's lifelong exercise program. They strike a middle way between an intense aerobic workout and doing nothing at all. Despite their gentleness, they "oil" the body by opening up the joints and relaxing tight muscles. Interestingly, recent scientific studies demonstrate that moderate and consistent exercise combined with some cardio-vascular effort is the key to better health and weight reduction for the majority of people.

Most of the movements are based on the idea of the circle rather than that of a straight line. An example of a straight-line exercise is the pushup which is designed to build up arm and shoulder muscles. Push-ups are aggressive and demanding of the body. The muscles are pumped up and compacted from the physical exertion of moving the weight up and down in a linear fashion.

Circular movements do not build up muscles. Their goal is to warm up the body in a gentle yet vigorous way. They open clogged veins and revive stagnant muscles. You will limber up rather than lumber up. The body is gradually stretched out, not contracted. One feels extension, the sweep of expanding limbs and torso. The body is given room to breathe and maneuver. The movement is something like the way a cat must feel when it stretches its body after a nap.

All movement contains aspects of contraction and expansion. Too much muscular contraction prevents us from opening up to life's vibrant impulses. Too much expansion prevents us from setting boundaries and defining direction. In my classes, often I see people suffering from chronic muscle contraction due to daily stress. The ideal movement in life as well as in physical exercise hinges on our ability to walk a Middle Path between chronic muscular contraction and endemic overextension. We can make changes in our unhealthy patterns by introducing alternative ways of movement that balance the extremes.

These warmups influence the body/mind in positive and subtle ways. I've found that they can soothe an angry soul and reduce the levels of tension. There have been times, for example, after a disagreement with my wife when I left the house angry on my way to teach a class. I have noticed that by the end of the lesson my anger has dissipated. From personal experience I believe that the combination of body and mind focus pulls me along The Middle Path, often without my being aware that it is happening.

These exercises are also designed to increase energy. After doing something sedentary like sleeping or reading a book, the body is cold and needs warming up similar to a car engine in the morning. Once started, the engine needs to idle for a few minutes before revving it up and demanding peak performance. Your body requires a gentle workout before it can operate at peak efficiency.

Within certain parameters, almost all exercise promotes better health. You might be surprised to learn that when you exercise, you actually engage in a kind of "oiling" process for the body. Exercise stimulates the healthy flow of the immune system's fluids. Along with meditation, regular exercise is one of the best ways to ensure that the immune system performs at its highest level. This is one of the best guarantees you can employ to protect yourself from debilitating illness.

The following exercises are easy to learn. They provide a healthy workout and yet do not cause undue stress on the body/mind. They also promote flexibility. This is absolutely crucial because these kinds of exercises arrest the inexorable stiffening and hardening of an aging body. This workout also lends itself to the special needs of the elderly or the disabled. In addition, they provide a good warm-up for practically any kind of physical activity from T'ai Chi to jogging. I recommend that you practice them when you get up in the morning, before you meditate or begin the exercises you will learn later on.

The Warm-up

Preparation:

Stand with your feet shoulder-width apart and parallel. The knees should be slightly bent and the body standing straight. Use the image of a string gently drawing the head upward. Breathe deeply until you feel relaxed and focused. If there are no numbers beneath the feet of the illustration, this means that the weight is evenly distributed. If you see numbers, they represent the approximate percentage of weight distribution. (Figure 1)

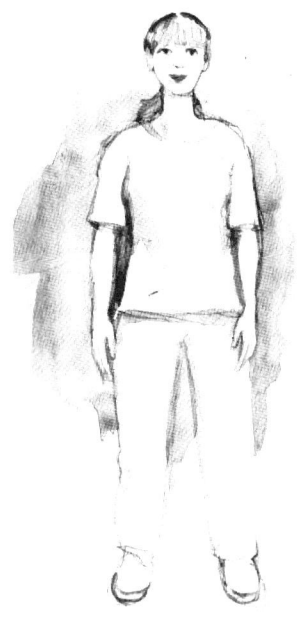

Figure 1

Stirring Heavenly Thoughts

This exercise loosens tight neck muscles

Figure 2a

1. Gently roll the head in large slow circles, first to the left 6 times and then to the right 6 times. If you feel dizzy, do less or stop. (Figure 2a)

2. Move the head toward the shoulders, side to side, beginning with the left, 6 times. (Figure 2b)

Figure 2b

3. Move the head backward and forward 6 times. (Figure 2c, and 2d)

4. Finish the head rolls by doing a few more circles in each direction. Ending with circles rounds the corners of tension in the body and promotes a feeling of relaxation.

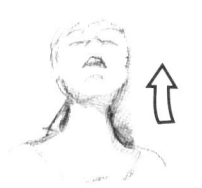

Figure 2c

Special Needs: If you have neck or head problems such as vertigo, do not do this exercise.

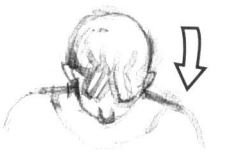

Figure 2d

Rolling the Shoulders

This exercise relaxes the shoulders and opens tight shoulder blades

1. First roll the shoulders forward into a large circle. Do this 6 times. (Figure 3a)

Figure 3a

2. Then reverse the shoulder roll, circling backward. Do this 6 times. (Figure 3b)

Figure 3b

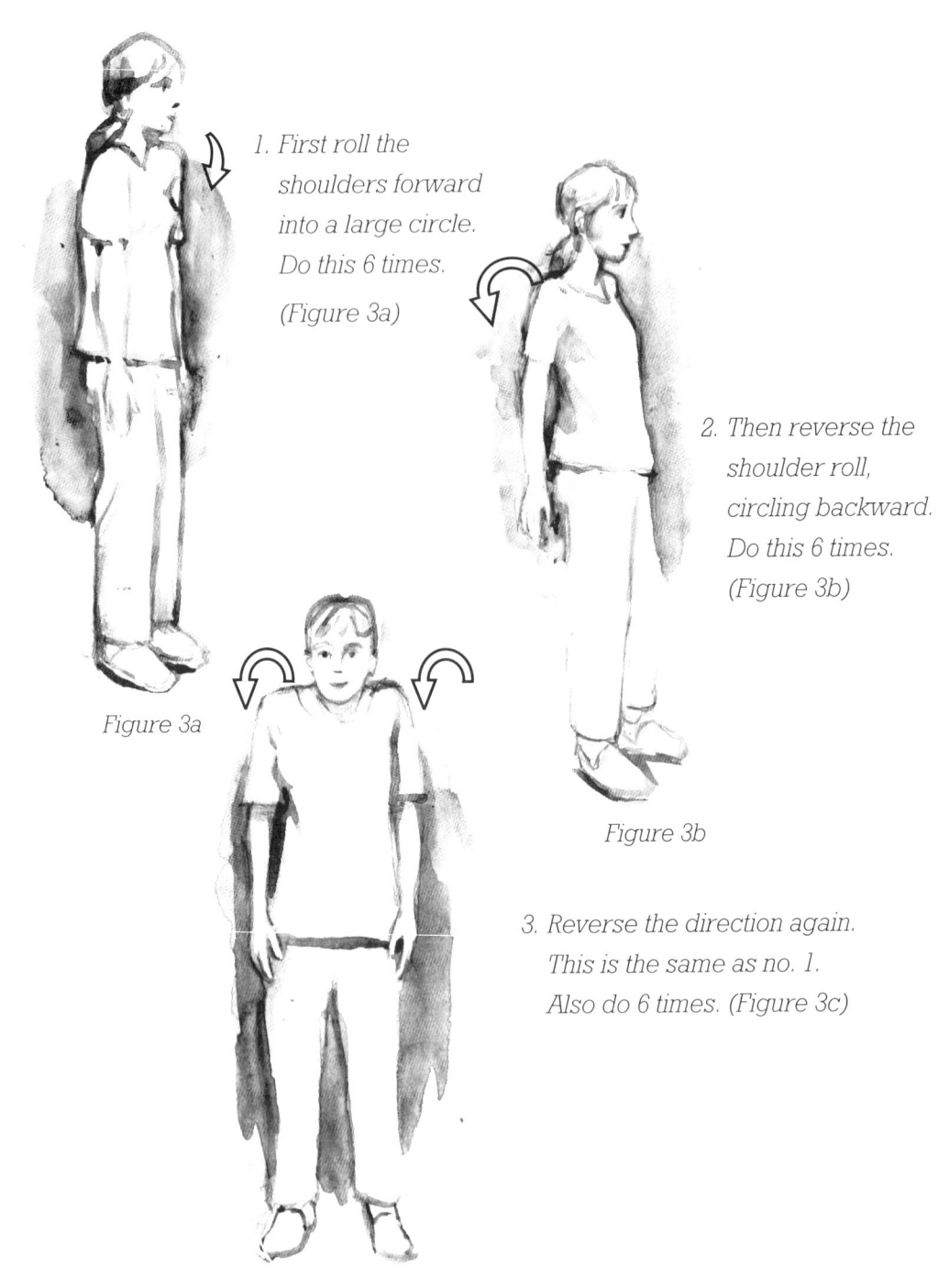

3. Reverse the direction again. This is the same as no. 1. Also do 6 times. (Figure 3c)

Figure 3c

A Warm Up for the Middle Path 31

The Propeller

In this exercise the legs and waist propel the sweeping movement of the arms. Practice and you will soon get the knack of it. Your body will flow in unison — arm, weight and waist. This exercise is particularly helpful in loosening and relaxing the shoulders, elbows and wrist joints. It also improves body coordination.

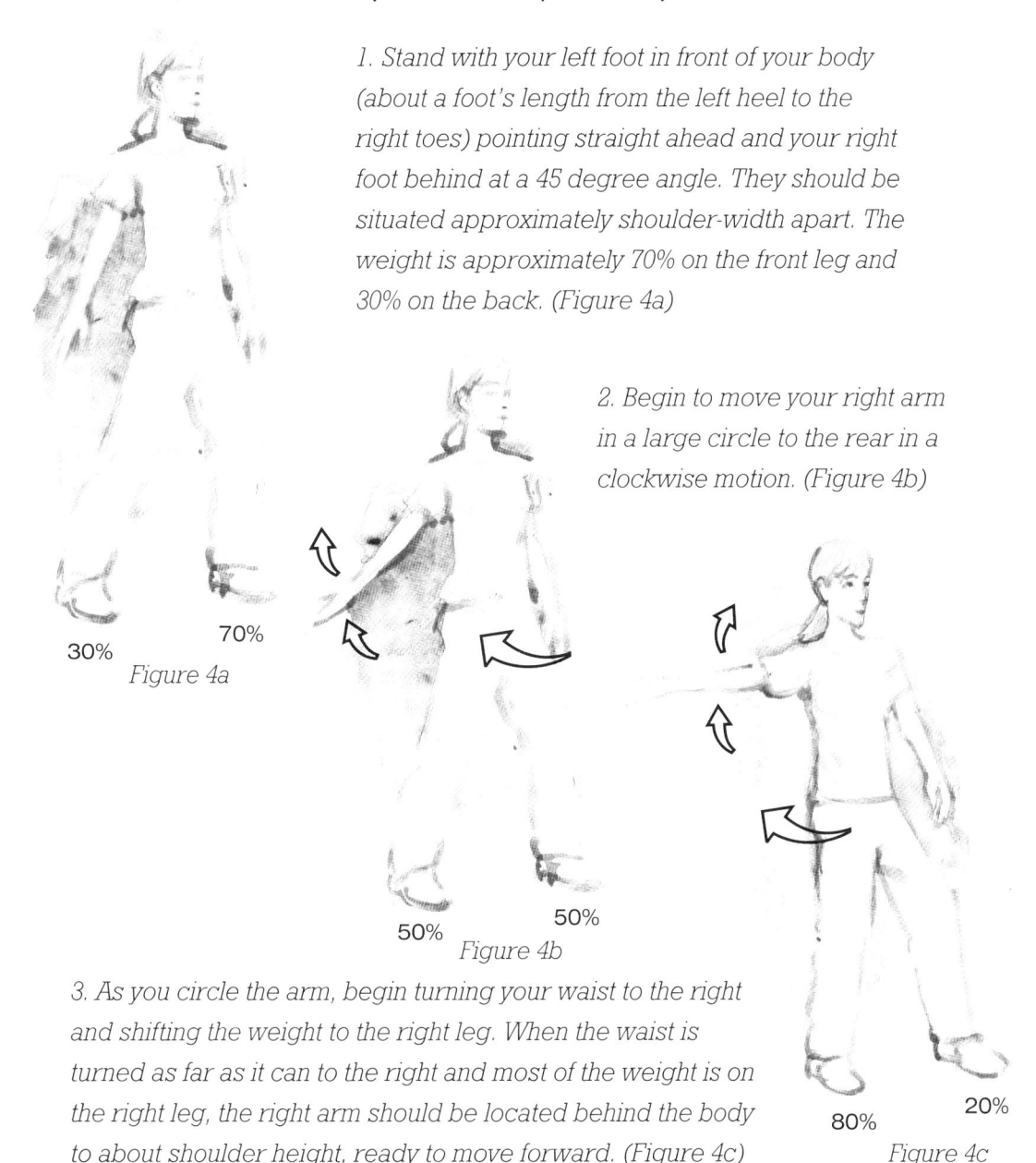

1. Stand with your left foot in front of your body (about a foot's length from the left heel to the right toes) pointing straight ahead and your right foot behind at a 45 degree angle. They should be situated approximately shoulder-width apart. The weight is approximately 70% on the front leg and 30% on the back. (Figure 4a)

30%   70%
Figure 4a

2. Begin to move your right arm in a large circle to the rear in a clockwise motion. (Figure 4b)

50%   50%
Figure 4b

3. As you circle the arm, begin turning your waist to the right and shifting the weight to the right leg. When the waist is turned as far as it can to the right and most of the weight is on the right leg, the right arm should be located behind the body to about shoulder height, ready to move forward. (Figure 4c)

80%   20%
Figure 4c

32 When Less Is More

4. As the arm circles forward, the waist gradually turns back to the center and the weight shifts to the front left leg (approximately 70%). (Figure 4d)

5. Do 6 circles to the front. Then reverse the circles and do 6 times to the rear. Finish with 6 circles to the front again.

6. Follow the same instructions for the other side.

Beating the Bodily Drum

The gentle pounding you will experience is good for opening up the stomach and chest. It also energizes the kidneys as it relaxes the lower back.

30%   70%
Figure 4d

1. Return to the stance of the feet being parallel and shoulder-width apart. The toes should be on the same line.

2. Turn the waist to the left as the weight also shifts to the left foot. The arms swing naturally to the left due to the momentum of the turning waist and the shifting weight. (Figure 5a)

3. The right palm gently slaps against the left hip and the back of the left hand slaps against the lower right side of the back. (Figure 5b)

4. Turn the waist and shift the weight to the right side, the hands slapping against the other side of the body.

5. As you swing from side to side, the hands and arms slap at different places on the body.

6. Do this 10 times on each side.

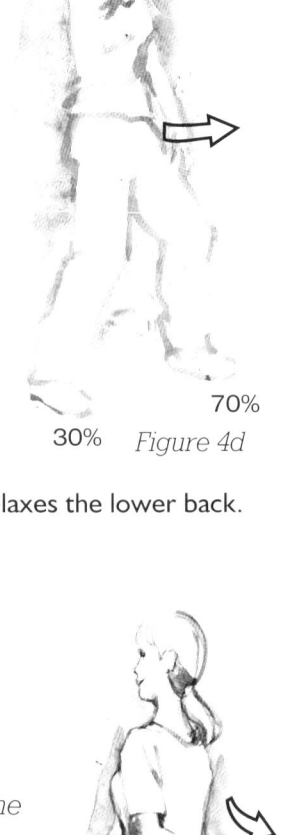

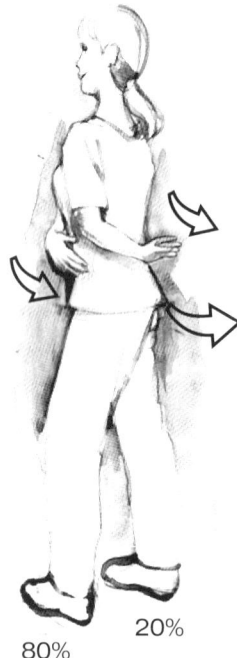

30%   70%
Figure 5a

80%   20%
Figure 5b

The Flower Blooms

In this exercise you can coordinate the breathing with the movement. Breathe in as the hands rise up to open and breathe out as the body and arms sink downwards. This exercise is particularly beneficial for opening the chest, lungs and heart.

1. Maintain the same stance as in the previous exercise, the feet parallel and shoulder- width apart. The arms hang naturally.

2. Begin by turning the hands inward so that the knuckles face one another (Figure 6a).

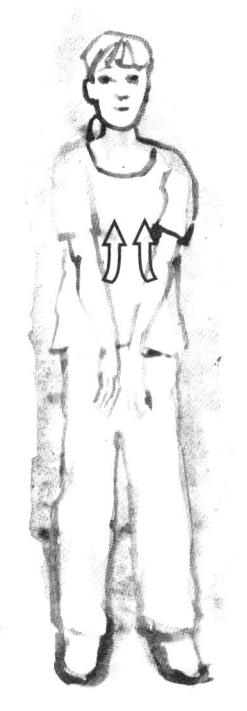

Figure 6a

3. Lift the hands upward along the centerline of the chest.

4. At the level of the neck they begin to turn palms up.

5. Once above the head, the hands stretch palms up with the head looking up. (Figure 6b)

Figure 6b

6. Then the arms trace a large circle and continue downward. At the same time the knees bend and the body folds over, the head leading the way with the pull of gravity (Figure 6c).

7. Be sure that you relax the neck downward.

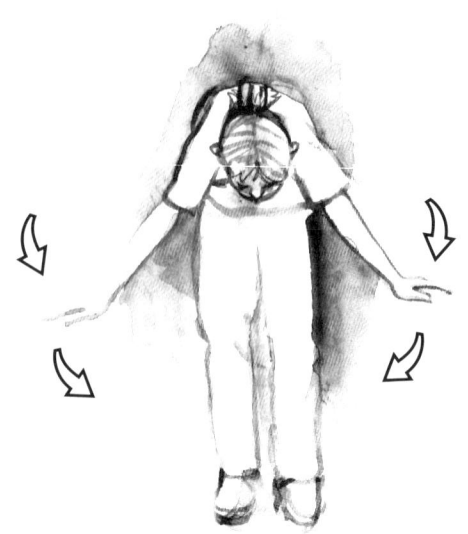

Figure 6c

8. When the hands reach close to the floor, the knuckles turn to face each other again and the hands rise along the centerline of the body (Figure 6d) as you gently begin to straighten yourself. The arms and hands continue to rise and then they open again.

9. Do this exercise 6 times.

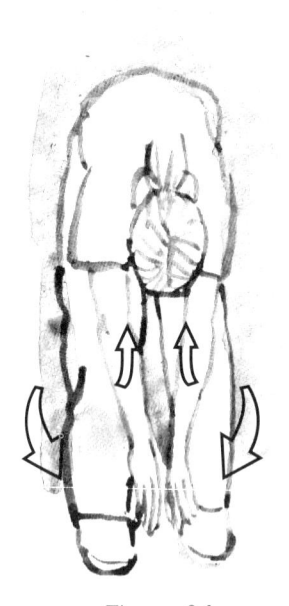

Figure 6d

Special Needs: You can do "The Flower Blooms" without bending over. At the level of the lower stomach, turn the knuckles so they face one another and raise the hands over the head. Then open them to the sides like a flower.

Reach for the Sky, Touch the Earth

The movement up stretches the body from the lower back to the fingertips, while bending over relaxes the lower back and limbers up the leg muscles. This exercise also relaxes the neck muscles.

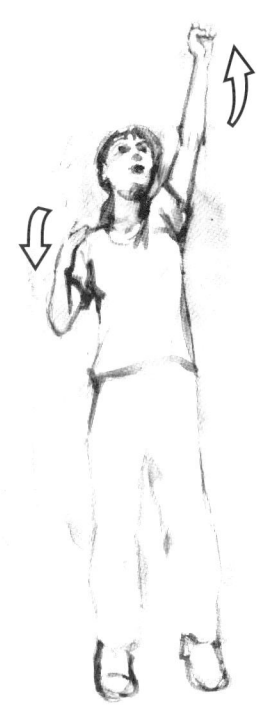

Figure 7a

1. In the same stance of shoulder-width with feet parallel, begin by stretching the left hand toward the sky and gradually closing it into a fist as if picking a piece of fruit. As the left descends, and opens, the right hand rises and does the same movement as the left, gradually forming a fist. (Figure 7a)

2. Your eyes should follow the rising hand. Feel your entire body stretch and open as your hands reach skyward.

Figure 7b

3. After 4 stretches, 2 on each side, with both hands and arms leading the way, lean to the left and lazily circle down until your arms are hanging straight down toward the ground. The head and neck should also be hanging down in a totally relaxed manner. The knees can be bent so that you can easily touch the ground. (Figures 7b and 7c.)

Figure 7c

36 When Less Is More

4. Hang in this position for at least 2 complete inhales and exhales of the breath. Be sure to keep breathing and try to stay relaxed.

5. Then, with your arms and hands, trace the same path up that you took to get in this position, that is, slowly raise your body up on the left side.

6. When you are standing straight, first stretch your hands skyward 4 times and then circle down to the right side.

7. Hang for 2 complete inhales and exhales of the breath. Come back up the right side.

8. Repeat this exercise at least a total of 4 times or 2 times to each side. If you feel dizzy, do not bend down all the way, or skip this exercise.

9. For a more intense stretch, when you are hanging, drop the buttocks as far as you can to the floor. (Figure 7d) Then, still touching the ground with your fingers and keeping the head down, raise the buttocks up by straightening the knees. Repeat this several times if you wish. This will stretch the muscles at the back of the legs. (Figure 7e)

Figure 7d

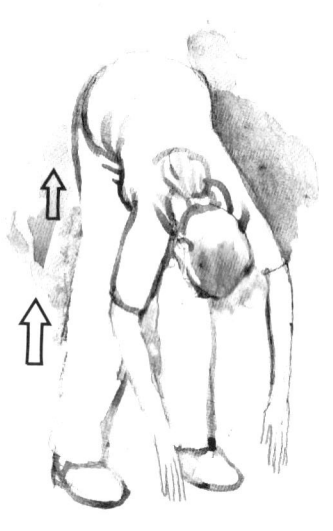

Figure 7e

Special Needs: Be careful with this exercise. Only do the stretching upward if you have back problems or difficulty bending over. My seniors often choose to modify this exercise by doing less.

Mixing the Chi of The Middle Kingdom

The goal of this exercise is to loosen up the waist and lower back. The movement is particularly helpful in opening the hip joints

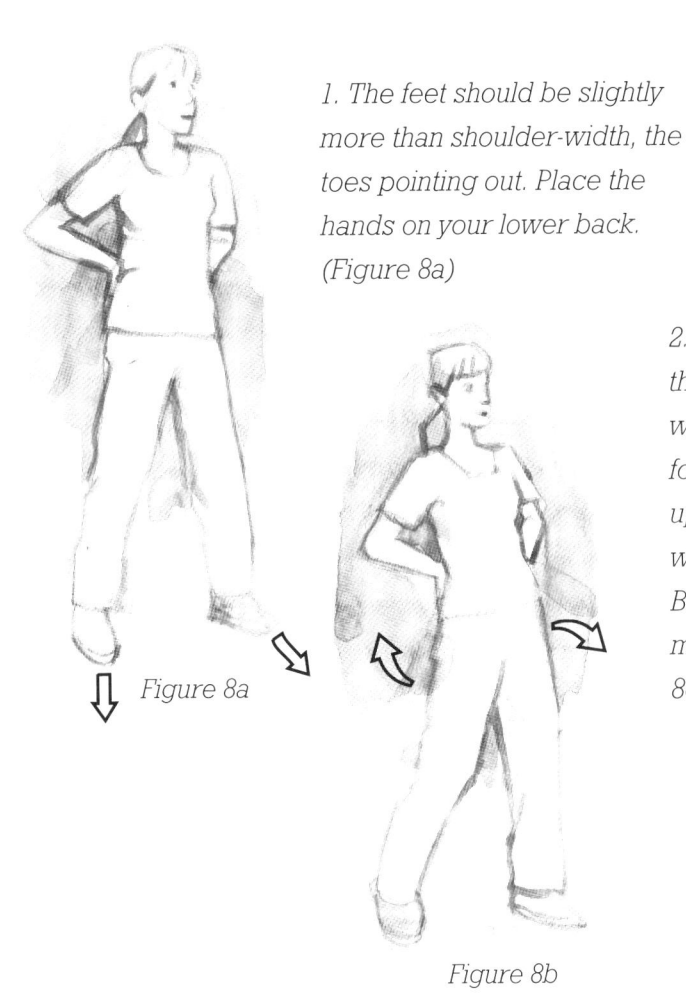

1. The feet should be slightly more than shoulder-width, the toes pointing out. Place the hands on your lower back. (Figure 8a)

Figure 8a

2. Begin circling the waist to the left, guiding the circle with your hands. You should focus on the waist. The upper body moves naturally with the turning of the waist. But the hips must lead the movement. (Figure 8b and 8c)

Figure 8b

3. Repeat 6 times and then circle to the right 6 times. If you wish, you can repeat the sequence.

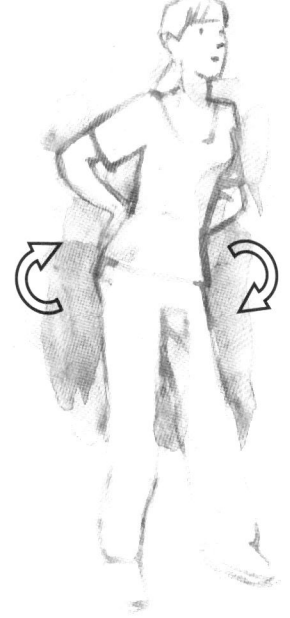

Figure 8c

Mixing the Lower Chi

This exercise strengthens the knees.

1. Bring the feet together so that they are touching. Bend over and place your hands on your knees.

2. Circle them to the left 6 times and then to the right 6 times. (Figure 9a)

3. Keep the feet flat on the floor.

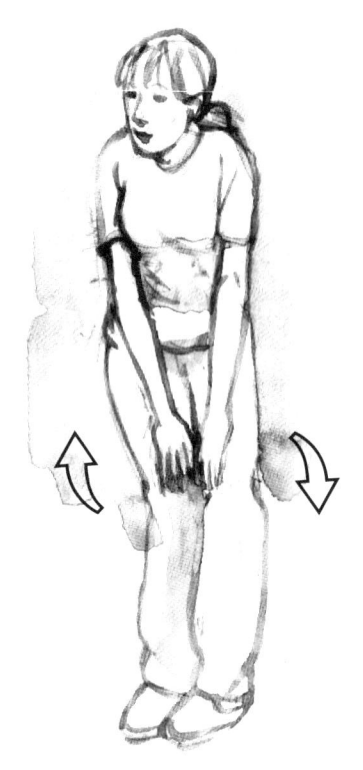

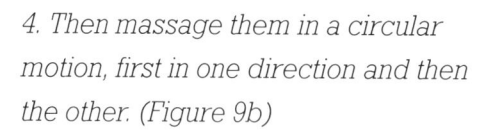

Figure 9a

4. Then massage them in a circular motion, first in one direction and then the other. (Figure 9b)

5. If you have knee problems, do less in the beginning. If you have any pain, skip this exercise.

Figure 9b

Special Needs: Do small circles, the smaller the better. Or simply massage the knees in a circular motion.

The Ladle Stirs the Soup

This is exercise helps to strengthen the legs and to develop better balance. It also opens the knee and ankle joints.

1. With hands on hips, stand on your right leg (Figure10a), begin slowly circling the left leg to the left 6 times and then to the right 6 times.

2. Simultaneously, the ankle also revolves around in a circle. (Figure 10b)

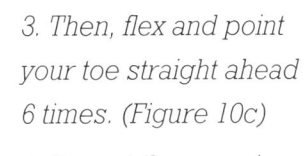

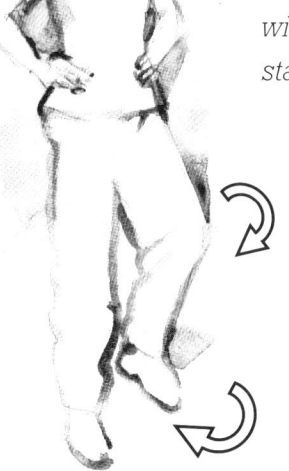

3. Then, flex and point your toe straight ahead 6 times. (Figure 10c)

4. Repeat the exercise with the right foot while standing on the left.

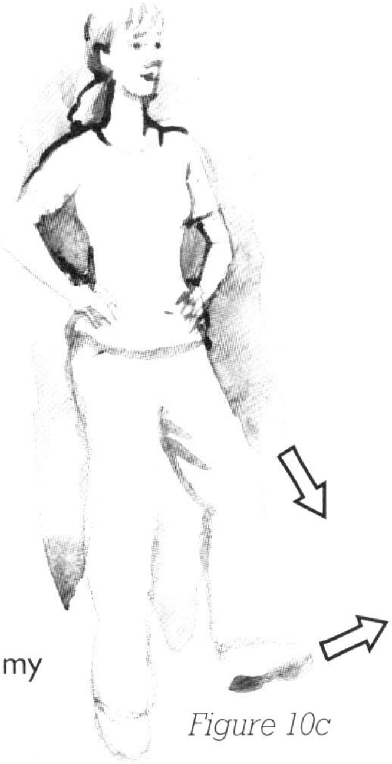

Figure 10a
100%

Figure 10b

Figure 10c

Special needs: Use a wall or a tree to stabilize yourself. In my special needs class, we hold hands in a circle for balance.

The author teaching a senior class The Ladle Stirs the Soup

Chapter 3

Meditation, Science, and The Middle Path

I never wanted to become a Buddha,

I wanted to become a man.

Cheng Man Ch'ing, T'ai Chi Master

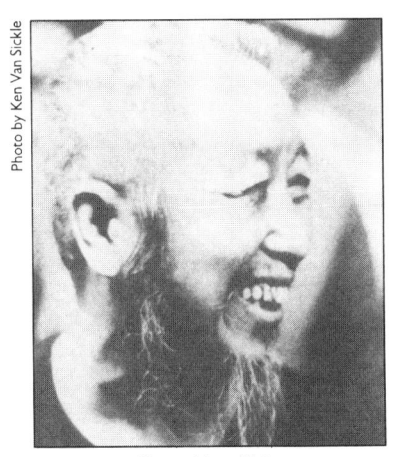

Cheng Man Ch'ing

Taming the Wild Horses

Cheng Man Ch'ing described the thoughts of the mind as a "herd of wild horses," running free without purpose. He believed that meditation is the way to rein in our thoughts and to put our will into the driver's seat. Meditation can tame our craving for lavish "wants". Once in control, we are in a position to understand who we really are and what our genuine "needs" are.

Meditation also helps us to be honest and truthful. When we meditate with sincerity, we must ask the same question of ourselves that God called out to Adam in the Garden of Eden: "Where are you?" We are also asking: "Who are you?" If we are honest and forthright, we do not conceal ourselves in a redolent garden of narcissistic thoughts. Instead, we answer the question by looking directly into ourselves. In a genuine encounter of meditation, we confront the image of God that dwells within us and, like a mirror on the wall that does not lie, we see ourselves as we really are.

Meditation and The Relaxation Response

While meditation is ultimately about truth and honesty, it also has demonstrable physical and psychological benefits for our health. These benefits are grounded in solid scientific research. The most well known study on the results of meditation emerged from the research of Dr. Herbert Benson, a cardiologist at Harvard University. His previous work with biofeedback and the reduction of high blood pressure established him as a leading researcher in his field.

In the late 1960s several followers of Transcendental Meditation approached him with the claim that they could lower their blood pressure through the practice of meditation. Transcendental Meditation (TM) teaches a simple easy-to-learn form of meditation that utilizes a mantra. Simply defined, a mantra is a word or a group of words repeated continually during the period of meditation. The mantra helps to free the meditator from thoughts and desires that hinder the process of calming the mind. It also focuses the mind by anchoring it in the present moment. Being totally present is a key ingredient in the art of successful meditation.

After some initial hesitation, Dr. Benson agreed to test their assertions under the probing light of scientific scrutiny. Dr. Benson and his colleague, R. Keith Wallace, reasoned that a quiet body and mind would lower the heart and breathing rates, which in turn should reduce their subjects' blood pressure. However, their assumption about the blood pressure in this initial group was incorrect as it remained about the same before and after meditation.

Why was the blood pressure of Dr. Benson's first group of meditators not lowered? He theorized that because of their TM experience, meditation could not lower their blood pressure any further. To test his theory, he recorded the blood pressure of 30 new applicants to TM. Dr. Benson then taught them a simple method of concentrating on the word "One." He asked them to meditate twice a day for six weeks. Most succeeded in reducing their blood pressure substantially. Moreover, when they stopped meditating regularly, their blood pressure began to rise.

From his research, Dr. Benson discovered that TM calmed the body and mind in a way that was different from the state when one merely sat quietly. Dr. Benson called this calm, meditative state, "The Relaxation Response." Dr. Benson speculated that the relaxation response could neutralize the hyperactivity of the sympathetic nervous system (fight-or-flight response) and thus promote better health by reducing the deleterious effects of rampant chronic stress. His book on the subject, *The Relaxation Response*, became a bestseller.

Dr. Benson's method contained four basic elements in order to achieve the relaxation response:

1) a quiet environment
2) a comfortable position
3) a passive attitude where thoughts are allowed to pass through the mind without holding on to them
4) a phrase or a sound to focus on

Dr. Benson's most recent book, *Timeless Healing*, goes a step further than his work with meditation. He believes that human beings by design are healthier when religious faith is added to the meditative equation. In a five-year study of people with chronic illnesses, he discovered that those who employed meditation and experienced a closeness to God through prayer enjoyed better health and made faster recoveries than those who only meditated. Dr. Benson speculated that prayer works along the same pathways of the human nervous system as the relaxation response. In a rather astonishing choice of words, he suggests: "...human beings are also wired for God." Of course, prayer, unlike meditation, requires the sincere belief that someone is out there listening.

The harmonious blending of meditation and prayer was common to the mystical traditions of all the major Western world religions, not to mention those of the East. In Islam we have the dervishes of the Jalladin Rumi's Sufi order; in Judaism, the mantra meditations of Abulafia and the "secluded prayer" of Rabbi Nachman; in Christianity, the Desert Fathers of the 4th and 5th centuries who sought to merge in a mystical union with the body of Christ. These are only a few of many examples.

Perhaps the apotheosis of meditation and prayer is best summed up in the psalmist's verse: "Let every breath of life praise God, Halleuyah!" "Breath" here can be understood to mean the breath of meditation, which is the door to the contemplative life.

Moses Maimonides, a key figure in our understanding of The Middle Path, also emphasized the connection of meditation and prayer. He observed: "True meditation is transcendent to prayer just as prayer is transcendent to sacrifice" Apparently, Maimonides believed that "true" meditation rested on a higher spiritual rung than prayer.

Many scientists have followed and expanded on the findings of Dr. Benson confirming the clear link between meditative states and improved health. For example, one researcher reported that the concentration of lactate in the blood of meditators decreases nearly 4 times as fast as people who are in an unfocused state of relaxation. A high level of blood-lactate is an indicator of anxiety or tension. This study also demonstrated that conscious effort in the act of meditation is different and more effective than merely resting or doing restful activities.

In another documented study on meditation, Dr. Gary E. Schwartz of Harvard University discovered a marked decline in psychosomatic disorders such as headaches and insomnia in meditators as compared to a control group of non-meditators. Significantly, Schwartz noted that meditators reported positive changes in lifestyle. For example, they decreased their consumption of alcohol and cigarettes.

Time magazine in June 1996 reported on a study showing that, among those who meditate, "75% of insomniacs begin to sleep normally, 35% of infertile woman become pregnant and 34% of chronic-pain sufferers reduce their use of painkilling drugs."

In 1976 Gurucharan Singh Khalsa conducted a pilot study at the Veteran Administration Hospital in La Jolla, California. His findings demontrated that a program of meditation and yoga increased the immune system's hormones by an amazing one hundred percent.

The above study confirms the similar recent results that Dr. Wen Zee, a Chinese cardiologist, observed in practitioners of T'ai Chi. T'ai Chi, like yoga, emphasizes exercise with focused meditation. Dr. Wen Zee tested a group of older people from age fifty to eighty, each of whom had at least twenty years of T'ai Chi experience. He took a blood sample before they practiced T'ai Chi, immediately afterwards, and then again two hours later. He discovered that immediately after T'ai Chi the T-cells in all the participants had risen to the level of a young person. After two hours they returned to a normal level, still unusually high for people of their age. While not conclusive proof, his study conveys a strong message that exercise combined with meditation strengthens the immune system.

In the 1980s, psychologist Alberto Villoldo of San Francisco State College demonstrated that meditation and self-healing visualization increased the response of white blood cells and the efficiency of hormonal response to physical stress. He employed a test of stress and pain by having his subjects place an arm in ice water. Dr. Villoldo discovered that those people trained in meditation could withstand the stress and pain of the ice water much better than those who did not meditate.

In another experiment, Dr. Villoldo found that two-thirds of the meditators could quickly stop the bleeding of an artery after a blood test by focusing their minds on the punctured area.

Similarly, Dr. Joan Borysenko, the author of *Minding the Body, Mending the Mind*, reported that diabetics could reduce their intake of insulin by using relaxation and meditation techniques.

Meditation can also reduce the levels of stress indicators in the body such as cortisol. This hormone increases the energy of the body during the fight-or-flight response, but it does so at the cost of inhibiting the strength of the immune system and the body's ability to repair tissue. In March of 1993 the *New York Times* reported on a study conducted by Dr. Kenneth G. Walton, a neurochemist on the staff of the Maharishi International University at Fairfield, Iowa. After four months, people taught Transcendental Meditation had lowered their cortisol levels by fifteen percent. An earlier study revealed that long-term meditators dropped their cortisol levels by twenty-five percent.

The New York Times also mentioned a study by a colleague of Dr. Walton's which showed that six hundred men and women in Quebec who meditated regularly for three years lowered their need for medical services on an average of twelve percent per year. Imagine how important his discovery is in this era of spiraling medical costs.

Visualization, an important part of meditation, is a powerful tool in focusing the mind to heal disease. Dr. Carl Simonton, a radiologist, is one of the pioneers in visualization and has documented some of the best known work in this field. In one case a 60-year-old man who had throat cancer could barely swallow and could no longer eat. Normally doctors label throat cancer at this advanced stage as "incurable." Dr. Simonton explained to his patient that visualization and relaxation techniques could strengthen his immune system. Through these techniques, it might be possible to inhibit the growth of his cancer. Dr. Simonton then taught the man how to relax deeply while picturing in his mind his immune system eliminating the cancer. After three months of treatment the patient recovered completely!

In another example, Dr. Bernie Siegel, the author of *Love, Medicine and Miracles* wrote about a young boy who had an incurable brain tumor. The boy imagined that spaceships were in his brain, shooting rayguns at his tumor. His cancer also disappeared.

These last two examples are powerful illustrations of the effectiveness of the Law of Transformation in healing: **Consciousness > Energy > Material World.**

Drs. Elmer and Alyce Green of the Meninger Clinic also reported a fascinating study on the use of visualization. Their patient was a man who was suffering severe pain from pelvic cancer. They hypnotized him and asked him to find the place in his brain that controlled the blood flow in his body. Then they asked him to find the veins that fed his tumor and turn off the flow. Within a few months the man's tumor shrank to one-fourth its original size. The man's pain disappeared and he left the hospital. Later, when he died of complications from surgery regarding another problem, his doctors discovered that the metastasized cancer had disappeared completely and the tumor had shrunk to the size of a golf ball.

Scientifically, the precise relationship of meditation to hypnosis is unclear at this point. However, most researchers in this field believe that meditation and hypnosis work along the same or similar pathways. Dr. David Spiegel, a professor of psychiatry at Stanford University, conducted therapeutic support groups for women with metastatic breast cancer. On average, the women in his groups lived about eighteen months longer than normally expected. Along with love and caring, Dr. Spiegel employed self-hypnosis as part of his therapy. He averred that hypnosis is "one highly structured way of regulating your inner states." Like meditation, hypnosis connects the individual to his or her inner life and enables a person to gain a modicum of control over it.

The above studies – and there are many others – reveal the quantitative results that meditation, prayer, visualization, and positive reinforcement systems can have on health when the mind exercises the body. They also confirm the valuable role that various forms of meditation can play as an antidote for chronic stress. When a meditator engages the relaxation response, the heart rate and blood pressure drop. The breath slows and deepens. The blood flow to the muscles decreases and the brain shifts from high gear to a more relaxed state. The nervous system is idling in neutral for a while, instead of driving at sixty miles per hour in first gear.

Meditation actually causes a change in brain-wave patterns from the normal beta waking state to an alpha pattern which researchers have correlated to a relaxed and calm frame of mind. These physical and attitudinal changes moderate the excessively competitive nature of the Type A personality and thus reduce the risk of heart disease. Meditation also increases the ability of people to cope with pain. When meditation is combined with physical exercise, it greatly magnifies the benefits to the immune system. Meditation is another way that the mind can exercise the body.

Meditation enables us to improve our health by creating an island of time in a turbulent sea of inner and outer space. We can forget our worries and tensions. Simultaneously we contact our "essential" selves in an honest and truthful way. We can listen to our internal compasses. Clearly meditation can be extremely important to a person's health and well-being. It is a healing balm that eases wear and tear on the body/mind while improving the quality of life.

Meditation and The Middle Path

Meditation is the gate to The Middle Path. It is an important tool by which we come to know ourselves, to bring our emotions into balance, and to avoid excess. Meditation improves concentration and helps us to become more centered in who we are.

How does meditation help us to know ourselves and by extension our true "needs"? The Chinese Buddhists of long ago had an interesting way of broaching this subject. They asked this simple question: "Is the host at home?" They were not inquiring about the proprietor of a hotel or the bon vivant of a gala party. By the "host," they meant something very personal and profound. They were speaking of the 'essential' person and not our public face as father, teacher or businesswoman. They were asking for the real person to stand up and be counted within his or her home, that is to say, within the body/mind. This is where the "essential person" is to be found. To know oneself is to journey to the heart of one's home. The art of meditation offers a method to find the host that dwells in you.

The word "host" was carefully chosen because it also implies certain responsibilities. The host is the one who is in charge of the home. This is in contrast to a guest who is simply visiting and has little or no responsibility. A guest is rarely as mindful or caring to the same extent as the host. A responsible host sets the tone and directs the activities in his or her home and property. He or she needs to be aware of all the goings-on.

Being a responsible host of the body/mind implies that "the buck stops here." It requires a commitment of awareness as to the direction and the character of our lives. Without a firm sense of who we are, we would soon lose our way and The Middle Path would be beyond our reach. Why is this so? Because The Middle Path exists as a reflection of our individual and unique natures. There is no such thing as an Abstract Middle Path that is suitable for all people. There is no map to tell everyone the way they should go. In practical terms, it exists only in relation to the needs of each individual. Thus, we must first know ourselves before we can find the way home.

When the host is at home, we can begin to see through pretense and superficiality. We can then reject the unwanted aspects of our personality that separate us from truth and genuineness. With awareness, we can descend to the deepest place in ourselves – to ground zero. This is the holy of holies of the human soul. There, we can learn who we are and what we want, to see things as they are and not as we wish them to be. This is where we will find our "internal compasses" that define the difference between "wants" and "needs." There, we can clearly ascertain what is ego gratification and what is essential for our lives to be whole. Once we are able to establish a genuine perspective of reality, we can begin to make sensible decisions concerning our lives.

In the beginning, getting to that private place is a delicate enterprise. It requires great sensitivity. We must weave a temporary cocoon around ourselves where we do nothing but observe the workings of the self, the comings and goings of our thoughts, and simply breathe deeply. This is a process of simplifying our outer activities and returning to basics. It is a way of gently coaxing the host back home.

By consciously seeking a quiet retreat for ourselves, within ourselves, we take the path that leads from the stress response to the relaxation response. In addition to calming us down, this process allows us to become aware of the attitudes, beliefs, and habits that empower daily stress to diminish the quality of our lives. Understanding the origins and dynamics of chronic stress is the starting point from where we can begin to resolve the problem. We become more mindful and aware of who we are, where we want to go and what is preventing us from getting there.

When we listen with our hearts, we unlock the hidden treasures of our own innate wisdom. We are wiser than we might think. Have you ever faced a difficult problem, gone to sleep and woken up the following morning with the answer? "It was so simple," you thought, "why didn't I think of it before?" Sometimes the best advice on solving a problem is to "sleep on it."

By the same token, when you have a problem, "meditate on it." Regular periods of conscious introspection can tap into hidden reserves of insight and allow the unconscious mind to reveal its wisdom. Hui-neng, one of the great Chinese Buddhist teachers, put it this way:

> *Whenever wisdom is active, calmness is within it.*
> *Whenever calmness is active, wisdom is within it.*
> *The two are one and the same.*

By meditating regularly, we become more centered and less easily influenced by outside sources. We have clear goals in life and are better able to stay on track to achieve them. Meditation helps to control self-defeating emotions such as anger, which can quickly push us off The Middle Path. Meditation can be a moderating force in our lives.

A recent incident drove this point home to me. Someone was preparing to pull out of a parking space. I maneuvered my car in front of the space and put it in reverse, ready to back in. This of course lit up the reverse lights in the back of the car as a signal of my intention. After the space was vacated, another car drove over the curb and into the space for which I was waiting. It was a flagrant act of discourtesy. At another time in my life, I would have been livid with anger. This time, relatively calm, I backed up and told the person in clear straightforward language that he had not followed the rules of the road or of common courtesy. He acted as though he did not understand what I was talking about. I drove on and found another parking place.

Later, as I walked by his car, I had to contend with feelings of incompleteness, of anger and the desire for revenge. Was I playing the fool in being too passive? The notion popped into my mind to take a coin and rake it across the side of his shiny new car. It would be so easy. But taking such revenge would be worse than his actions. I laughed to and at myself for entertaining such a satisfying yet wrongheaded and petty idea. Fortunately, good sense prevailed and I walked on. In that instance, I am certain that the quiet afterglow of many sessions of meditation walked with me.

Meditation can help us to find The Middle Path and better health. It helps us to relax and put our worries on hold. When we meditate, we place our awareness in the middle of the present moment. Temporarily, we have no past and no future. This is not a time for scheming or making money or doing most of the things we are busy with during the normal activities of the day. Instead, we stop and sink to the center of our being. This is the way of meditation and the means to The Middle Path. This is the training ground of Wu Wei where well-timed and spontaneous actions spring from still waters deep within ourselves.

When we meditate, we try to remain nonjudgemental toward the thoughts or resistances that may surface. This impartiality encourages an open mind and an acceptance of others and their opinions. The whole process is one of inviting harmony and balance to congregate in the halls of our consciousness. Through periods of quiet meditation, we can nurture a more sane and healthy perspective on life. As an antidote to a jaded view of reality, we return to what is real in ourselves, to feel our own natural rhythms, and to listen to the song of our hearts.

Often we find ourselves in conflict with what we do in daily life. We experience a general malaise of unease: that something is amiss even though everything seems outwardly fine. The problem is that we are playing a role in a drama that is not ours, where we haven't a clue who the director is or who is writing the script. Meditation is an odyssey into inner space where we travel the byways of our own minds. It is a way of contacting our unique inner vision and a way of discovering how we want to conduct our lives.

Through meditation, we seek to focus the mind's concentration. It is an antidote for the "butterfly effect" where the mind constantly skips from one idea to the next. Ordinarily we waste a great deal of energy due to a lack of focus. The word "meditation" literally means "to measure or to weigh in the act of contemplation." It is a process of learning to see ourselves as we really are and thus we are able to keep things in proportion.

One important goal of meditation is to allow our mind to calm down and to settle naturally into place. One famous Chinese Confucian, Chu Hsi, described the mind as a beautiful pearl lying at the bottom of a muddy pond. When the mud settles, we can clearly see the pearl's beauty. Meditation allows the unclear static in and around the body/mind to settle down. It represents a call to order, where one organizes, galvanizes, and directs the diverse elements of life. It is a way of keeping perspective on the various competing interests that contend for our attention. In this way we ensure that the chaos of conflicting demands do not overwhelm us. This is an important step in combating chronic stress. Meditation teaches patience and how to maintain balance, no matter what the external circumstances are. We become the master of our emotions.

In the beginning meditation does not always go smoothly. Many conflicting emotions may surface in the form of memories and feelings that we have suppressed for years. We are accustomed to the noise and bustle of constant activity. Suddenly, we are asked to sit quietly and watch our breath. This can be nerve-wracking because it signals a major shift from our normal reality. Without warning, we must lower the protective armor that shields us against unwanted intrusions from the outside world. By letting down our guard, we naturally feel naked and self-conscious, not unlike modern versions of Adam and Eve. We wonder, "What should I be thinking?" "My legs are hurting." "I feel claustrophobic." "Let me out of here." These and many other obstacles will confront the beginner during meditation.

In my classes I have noticed that people have certain expectations about what it means to meditate. It scares them and makes them nervous. For that reason, I am sometimes hesitant to use the word "meditation." Instead, I substitute the words, "relaxation techniques." For many people, meditation conjures up an image of monks in saffron robes, sitting long hours in perfect silence as incense smoke wafts about them. While this exotic image has an allure for some people, it does not resonate with the inclinations of most Westerners. They simply want to improve the quality of their lives in a practical way.

Fortunately, with patience and perseverance, most people will overcome these hindrances and prejudices. After a period of consistent practice, they will experience a genuine sense of well-being, expressing itself in daily life. But this sense of well-being cannot be built in a day. Even if you feel peaceful after the first day of meditation, it is probably the calm before the storm. When the storm comes, don't give up! Be patient and stay with your practice. In the early days of meditating, the true challenge lies in "the doing" and doing it consistently. It might be worthwhile to find a group in your area that meditates on a regular basis to keep your practice consistent. Being consistent and cultivating regular habits are important qualities to nurture as you journey along The Middle Path of meditation.

The beauty of the meditations, visualizations and exercises in this book is that they neutralize the dire effects of chronic stress. They succeed in this by harmonizing and integrating the subtle relationships of the entire body/mind organism. These exercises actively engage the body and the mind and encourage them to work together in natural harmony. This is particularly true of the series of exercises known as Ch'i Kung. With the steady and deep rhythms of the breath, the body moves and the mind mellows. Motion and stillness are integrated. Chronic stress melts away like the black of night when a candle is lit.

How does this work? When you are in motion, that is to say, active in the world, perhaps doing Ch'i Kung or at your job, you must do many things at once. The unity that you feel when meditating naturally separates. Yet unity and separation are actually two aspects of the same reality like the ocean and its waves. The great value of meditation is that it remains with you even when you are active. The reverse is also true. When you meditate, there is still motion, for example, your breath. The world does not stop when you meditate. Rather you have woven the various layers of existence into one fabric. You have touched a different reality.

Walking The Middle Path with meditation as your companion will help you to become a more integrated and healthy human being. This is a reachable and ultimately practical goal. As with anything worthwhile, you must commit yourself to discipline and hard work. At the same time, you will embark on an exhilarating and often mysterious journey that leads toward self-knowledge. It is an odyssey where you will begin to expand your boundaries and to realize your full potential as a human being.

Practical Exercise:

Finding Your Internal Compass: The Spirit Guide

The following meditation is particularly useful in helping a person to tap into his or her innate wisdom. The central focus of this meditation, the spirit guide, is a kind of higher self that dwells in the unconscious mind. The meditation itself is a device to melt the ice between different parts of the human psyche. For many people, the conscious and unconscious minds are like neighbors who occupy different rooms in the same house but share only a nodding acquaintance. Contacting one's spirit guide enables a person to establish a link between intuitive wisdom and conscious awareness.

When you are learning this exercise, it might be helpful to have a friend read these instructions out loud and guide you through them. You can also tape your own voice as a guide. Before you initiate this meditation, formulate a clear question or questions in your mind that you would like answered.

Sit comfortably, close your eyes, breathe deeply. When you are relaxed, in your mind's eye take a walk on a path that leads through a beautiful green meadow lush with the golden flowers of spring. Relax! There is no hurry. You can amble along at a leisurely pace. Stop and smell the flowers. Notice the soft blue sky, the warm sun above, billowing white clouds lazily drifting across the sky, and a refreshing gentle breeze gusting from time to time. Enjoy your walk. Gradually the meadow leads into a rich forest of evergreens, spruce, and eucalyptus. Birds are flitting from tree to tree, their song echoing across the forest's floor. In time, the trees give way to a clearing along the way. There is a small brook bubbling nearby. (You can use any scene from nature that leads you to your spirit guide.)

You notice that someone is sitting in the clearing. You walk slowly up to the person and sit down beside him or her. There is a sense of recognition. Yet you know intuitively that you do not have to say a word. The silence is restful, easy, and reassuring. You feel that this person is someone who is wise and unpretentious, someone you can trust with your innermost thoughts and feelings. You feel safe, that he or she will respect whatever you do or say. Time passes and you feel ready to speak. You request permission from your spirit guide to ask a question. If he or she answers affirmatively, then ask your question.

Listen carefully to what he or she says or does. The answer may ring out clear as a bell or be mysterious like a riddle. When your spirit guide finishes, thank him or her. When you feel ready, slowly rise and begin to walk back the way you came through the same meadow. Take your time walking back and enjoy each precious moment of your journey. Notice the sky, the trees, and the breeze. Pay attention to any changes in your return journey, not just in nature but also in yourself.

When you feel the meditation nearing completion, gradually return to your normal waking self. Focus on your breath and relaxing your body. When you feel ready, open your eyes. Because your experience is still fresh in your mind, you should carefully ponder your spirit guide's answer. Write it down. His or her message may contain a solution to your problem or, at the very least, a direction to follow. If the answer rings true to the wisdom of your intuition, it is usually the right one. You will know it! You might feel that the answer was so obvious that you knew it all along. If you have doubts about the answer, it will still give you food for thought.

With some experience, you will be able to approach your spirit guide without going through an involved meditation. You will simply ask and usually receive an immediate answer. But you must **remember** to ask! There will be no clear answers without formulating clear questions.

Try this meditation. You need not feel bound to the above scene. Create your own story. My imagery comes from a park in Marin County near San Francisco. This meditation has provided me with a wealth of wisdom and guidance. The spirit guide has given birth to many important decisions in my life.

Chapter 4

The Seven Steps to Better Health Through Meditation

A Journey of a thousand miles begins with the first step

Chinese Folk wisdom

1. Preparation
> 2. Posture
>> 3. Focus
>>> 4. Breath
>>>> 5. Centering
>>>>> 6. Letting go
>>>>>> 7. Visualization

1. Preparation

You plant the seeds of success or failure in most endeavors, according to the level of your preparation. This is particularly true for beginning meditators. With this in mind, you should strive to create the right atmosphere that will be optimally conducive for arousing the relaxation response. Assign yourself a specific time, preferably twice a day, morning and evening, to practice. It is also wise to choose a special place where you are comfortable, one that is not too hot or too cold, where the lights can be dimmed, the air is fresh, and quiet pervades the room. Unplug the phone or put on the answering machine with the voice off.

Do not let anything prevent you from your practice except an emergency. This is your special time when you are doing something important for your well-being. Be reasonably selfish in this. Do not be deterred.

Your clothing should be comfortable and loose. Remove all jewelry and glasses, anything that feels heavy and distracting. Do not practice immediately after meals or the drinking of alcohol.

If you are ill or not feeling up to par, listen to your body and do less. But try to do something. Pay attention to the warning signs of dizziness, excessive fatigue, heart palpitations, pain, or strange thoughts. Just stop if things do not feel right and try again later.

Be moderate, gentle, and considerate of yourself. Know your limits, keep practicing; and remember: a little progress each day is the key, not occasional leaps and bounds followed by doing nothing. In the cultivation of any activity, it helps to practice the virtues of patience, consistency and perseverance.

Your attitude is very important. Keep your expectations low and your determination high. If you come to meditation with high expectations, you will probably find yourself disappointed. The kiss of death for a film is somebody telling you beforehand that it was the greatest movie they ever saw. What movie could possibly live up to this kind of accolade? The same is true for meditation.

The best attitude for meditation is not to expect anything. Focus your awareness on the simple things of your experience. Be aware of the gentle, deep rhythms of your breath. Nothing could be more pedestrian than breathing: we do it all the time. Perhaps this is why we undervalue it. Yet paradoxically, this commonplace, often involuntary activity is one of the most important signs that we are alive.

Focus on being present in the moment, in the here and now. Follow the instructions of each exercise and forget about achieving anything. Allow the psychological and physical health benefits of meditation to gradually unfold on their own accord. Give yourself a break and trust the meditation.

2. Posture

Modern culture accepts the intimate connection of body and mind to such an extent that the word 'body/mind' has become part of our vocabulary. Today few realize that this is a revolutionary concept. The influence of body and mind on each other is immensely complicated and intricately entangled. To speak of them as being separate can be misleading and fallacious. Yet it is often necessary to begin with one in order to elicit positive change in the other. Posture is an excellent example of this.

In the practice of meditation, poor posture will influence the mind and limit the effectiveness of the meditation. On the other hand, clarity in one's posture will increase the likelihood that there will be clarity in one's mind. Slouching, for example, encourages the mind to wander. Sitting or standing stiffly will cause the body to rebel with symptoms of a sore back or neck. It can also cause the mind to cling to fixed patterns.

Beginners often complain about soreness in their backs. People commonly carry a lot of tension in their bodies. To cope with this discomfort, they hold themselves in stiff postures as a way to mask the tension or pain. I have one student who hurt his back some years before and found that by tightening his buttocks, his groin, and lower back, the pain was reduced. But this method was wreaking havoc because it was causing tension throughout his whole body.

Pain is simply a reality-check of what is happening in your body. Meditation is not the cause of the pain. It is bringing your discomfort to the forefront and allowing you to see (feel) it. For the vast majority of people, with time and regular meditation, the soreness will disappear as the tension dissipates.

The following are basic postural instructions: Whether doing sitting or standing meditation, (Chap. 6) hold the spine erect, with the head directly over it, as if the top of the head is being drawn toward the sky by a string. Relax the shoulders, chest, and stomach downwards as the head gently lifts up toward the ceiling. As we grow older, the spine and neck have a tendency to collapse with the pull of gravity and the weakening of the body. The notion of lifting the top of the head with the image of the string is an important counterbalance to this damaging tendency. This way of sitting or standing is effective in countering osteoporosis.

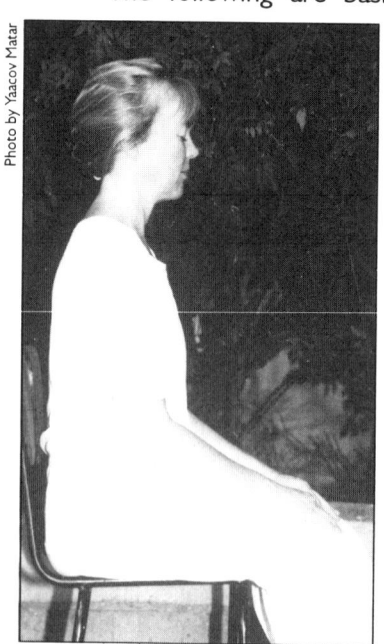

Tuck in the chin slightly as the ears and shoulders line up, more or less vertically. Your body

Photo by Yaacov Matar

should be upright, and not leaning in any direction.

These postural instructions are valuable to put into practice in almost all situations, whether working on a computer or watching television. At the same time, you are not a stiff statue, but a living being of flesh and blood. So, within the posture, remember to relax! Try to find softness and roundness within the integrity of an upright posture. Like a parent who must be firm with his child, disciplining your own body/mind must come from a sensitive place of love and compassion.

If you are sitting, place your hands on the top of the thighs or fold them in your lap. Your feet should be resting flat on the floor. Gently close or partially close your eyes. Soften your eyes so that you are not staring intensely at anything in particular.

Beware of lying down to meditate. This is a quick way to fall asleep. Moreover, studies show that meditation engages the relaxation response much better than sleep. Sleep and meditation are two very different activities. We need plenty of both.

3. Focus

An age-old problem of anyone who works with the mind is the problem of focus. How does one get the mind to do what you want it to do? It seems that the mind has a "mind" of its own. When one sits down to concentrate, often random thoughts appear and run wild. You might find yourself recounting the events of the day. You might be considering what you will eat for dinner or you might be feeling like an idler wasting time. Wandering thoughts are normal and should be taken with a grain of salt. Once again, be easy with yourself. The Christian mystic, St. Francis de Sales (d. 1622) offered this sage advice:

> *If the heart wanders or is distracted, bring it back to the point quite gently...And even if you did nothing during the whole of your hour but bring your heart back, though it went away every time you brought it back, your hour would be very well spent.*

"Gently" is the key word here. De Sales also encourages perseverance. He well understood the problem of fixing one's concentration on a single idea – in his case, that of God. For us, the solution is to bring the mind back to its objective, whether it be watching the breath or observing one's thoughts, *gently and persistently*. It's something like teaching a puppy to sit or to stay. You have to be firm and persistent until the puppy finally gets it. Using excessive force will be counterproductive to the spirit and will probably drive the mind into a cantankerous state of rebellion. Don't be frustrated. Just stay with your daily practice.

Teachers of meditation are well aware of the dilemma of focusing the mind. Suzuki-Roshi, the late Zen master who taught in San Francisco, said that "the best way to control people is to encourage them to be mischievous..." He used the analogy that one should give a sheep or a cow a large, spacious meadow in order to control him. In other words, give the mind a wide field to roam in and just watch it. Let your thoughts come and go as they will. When they have nothing to fight against, such as your insistence that they go away, they will settle down on their own. Simply focus on your breath and observe what is going on moment to moment. Nothing more. Do not feel guilty because your mind will not do your bidding. It is only temporary. Even experienced meditators go through periods when their minds will not settle down.

There are two basic ways of focusing the mind. In the first method the meditator concentrates on a single object to stop the mind from wandering. When Dr. Benson had his subjects say the word "One" as a mantra, he was employing a venerable method of mind-focusing. The Zen tradition has beginning students focus only on the inhale and exhale of the breath. Other methods seek similar results through visualization. The Lamaze system of birth, for example, teaches mothers to place their attention on a focal point outside the body. The idea is that this focus will distract her from the pain of giving birth.

The second method to improve concentration is to focus on the various sensations, feelings, and mental states as they arise in the mind from moment to moment. This is a way of centering the mind in the "here and now." It promotes a sense of being genuine and of partaking in an authentic experience of reality. When we are sitting quietly and focusing only on our physical sensations, we naturally feel that they are real and that we are involved with a process of being real. If we are feeling pain or discomfort, we know that there is nothing phony about it.

In this second way of focusing, it is important to remain an "objective observer." Granted, it is not easy to remain detached and objective when one is experiencing pain or, on the other hand, thinking pleasurable thoughts. Nevertheless, there is much to be gained from imposing this kind of discipline on the mind. By not becoming entangled with our sensations or thoughts, they gradually lose their power over us. A good deal of what goes on up there is simply useless mind-chatter. Moreover, when we learn to eliminate much of our internal chatter, our minds become more efficient tools that respond to the will of our intentions. Our minds, and therefore our lives, become more streamlined.

We should not become overly invested or caught up in the process of meditation or relaxation exercises. We must find The Middle Path between excessive enthusiasm and spiritless ennui. When you practice focusing, treat your sessions as something ordinary. Do not make them into a big deal or put any undue pressure on yourself. This is a good way to prevent unrealistic expectations.

I chuckled at a cartoon that I saw recently. Two monks are sitting together after meditating. The younger one looks over to the older one and asks: "'Is that all there is?'"

In matters of the mind there is often more work than fireworks. The Zen tradition emphasizes that even after enlightenment, outwardly things remain the same. This is a way to ensure that egos filled with "too much" enlightenment do not get out of hand. Suzuki-Roshi explained remaining "nothing special" in this way:

> *It is kind of a mystery that for people*
> *Who have no experience of enlightenment,*
> *Enlightenment is something wonderful.*
> *But if they attain it, it is nothing. But yet it is not nothing....*
> *For a mother with children, having children is nothing special.*

What Suzuki-Roshi left unsaid was that for the mother, having children is also something special. Similarly, developing a deeper awareness of our reality is a very special accomplishment. Yet once achieved, it becomes ordinary. A life of focused awareness constantly revolves around plateaus of the commonplace and peaks of the fantastic. We become aware that a different reality can be just a breath away.

In focused meditation we strive to stay aware and conscious of what is actually happening. We pay attention to the breath because it is a grounding element that maintains our link to our inner reality and to life itself. We make mental notes of our experiences but try to stay detached from them. Simultaneously, we are engaging the relaxation response in order to bring our sympathetic and parasympathetic nervous system into balance. Although focusing primarily begins with the mind, we also work on the body. As emphasized before, the body/mind is a concept of unity. When we focus on one, we influence the other.

4. Breath

All cultures recognize the importance of the breath. It is the gate that links our inner world to the world of everyday experience. Breath is often synonymous with the word "Spirit": in Sanskrit, it is called prana; in Greek, pneuma; in Latin, spiritus; in Hebrew, ruach. In Chinese, the word Ch'i, which originally was defined as breath, also means the "life-force" of the universe. In Genesis God created Adam by *breathing* life into his lungs. We can do without food, water or love for an extended period, but we cannot stop breathing for a few minutes and still live.

The cultures of East and West viewed the breath as the fundamental link between the unconscious and conscious mind. The manner in which we breathe is a microcosm of who we are and reflects the condition of the larger body/mind system. It is an important indicator of who and where we are. In the whisper of our breath, we hear the eternal, ever-recurring echo of the ancient question that God put to Adam: 'Where (who) are you?'

Watching the breath while meditating pulls the meditator into the present moment, the now of forever. The watcher cannot catch his or her last breath and cannot know whether there will be a breath in the future. The only certainty is the breath of the moment. That breath is real!

The breath has its own language. The quality of one's breathing can point to a hidden world that lies beneath the surface of human interaction. The breath functions like a revolving door that opens and closes with each inhale and exhale, linking the inner experience with the outer world. It is a dynamic interplay of action, response, and reaction. The way one breathes intimates not only the underlying psychological state of the person, but also suggests the nature of his or her social relationships.

In everyday language, if someone fails to come through during a crucial moment in sports, we say: "he choked." This phrase suggests that not breathing freely led to a tightening up of the body and a failure to put the ball through the hoop or to get a hit in baseball. With regard to emotions, we also say: "Someone is choked up with grief."

It follows that we should be able to improve our physical and psychological state if we can learn to breathe properly. There is a strong and vital nexus between the quality of breathing and the strength of our "grounding." Breathing properly can also help us to relax and improve the way we relate to the world. Deep focused breathing is a sign that someone has achieved a degree of tranquility. Lao Tzu understood this power of the breath when he wrote:

Can you keep body and soul always focused so they do not stray?
Can you regulate the breath and become open (innocent) like an infant?

People who suffer from chronic stress have overly stimulated sympathetic nervous systems. With regard to the breath, two types of symptoms manifest themselves: rapid and shallow breathing or short and tight breathing. The former reflects an excessively expansive way of breathing while the latter indicates an excessively constricted type of breathing. Both extremes signal that the autonomic system is out of whack and in dire need of balancing. If not tended to, the person's eco-system will eventually suffer serious damage.

A balanced person who is "grounded" will breathe naturally in a way that is neither overly expansive nor overly constricted. Through the breath, he or she will be in touch with an inner flow of personal vitality that merges harmoniously with the outer ocean of aliveness. The two energies, inner and outer, are the same and, like a grand canal that ties one ocean to another, the breath links them together.

Breathing techniques have the facility to heal and to counter the ill-effects of chronic stress. Breathing can calm the person who is experiencing extreme and constant pressure. By breathing in a deep and relaxed manner, one can actually break the cycles of fear and helplessness. Indeed sometimes the best advice for someone laboring under such adverse circumstances is to stop, relax, and take a few deep breaths.

Even if a person has the time and the will to stop and breathe, there is a right way and a wrong way to go about it. In the West we have the alluring image of the muscle man with a bulging chest, massive arms, and a flat rippling stomach. But how healthy is this person? One of the major problems of this muscle-bound physique is that it inhibits the free-flow of deep abdominal breathing and thus promotes shallow breathing. The excessive constricted breathing of the muscle builder may prevent him or her from experiencing and penetrating the world in a tender and sensitive way. The hardened muscles form a kind of shell that prevent deep inner feelings from being expressed outwardly.

At the other end of the spectrum, there is the laughing Buddha whose stomach is ample enough for three people. While we may not want bellies as large as his, he nevertheless expresses a sense of joy and well-being derived in part from his ability to breathe deeply and uninhibitedly from the belly. The laughing Buddha symbolizes Eastern practices of meditation that encourage the naturally rhythmic expanding and contracting of the belly with the breath. Indeed, meditators of old described the entire body as being a vessel for the breath. They inhaled and exhaled through their fingers and toes. They consciously choreographed body, breath, and mind to move together in quiet harmony. Mok Lau, a seventy-year-old modern Ch'i Kung master, described proper breathing in this way:

> *Breathing is like playing the piano. You can go over to the piano and hit the keys. You'll have notes but no music. But if you organize the notes with timing and highs and lows and thoughts, it becomes a melody.*

"Abdominal breathing" is far more beneficial than breathing only with the lungs. It is the classical form of playing music with your breath. It is also the healthiest and most calming way to breathe. Abdominal breathing is deep and rhythmic, and helps to engage the relaxation response. If we can breathe abdominally in a natural way throughout the entire day, we can create an ever-present natural inhibitor to the dangers of chronic stress. But first we must learn how to breathe properly and then practice it during moments of meditation.

The key to abdominal breathing lies with the diaphragm, which is a group of muscles located beneath the lungs and shaped like a skullcap. The diaphragm is an extremely sensitive indicator of our mental state. If it is tight and sore, this is a sure sign that we are suffering some kind of stress. If it moves freely, this suggests that the person is relatively stress free. The good news is that, through grounding techniques and focusing on our breath, we can relax the diaphragm over time and thereby create a better balanced body/mind eco-system.

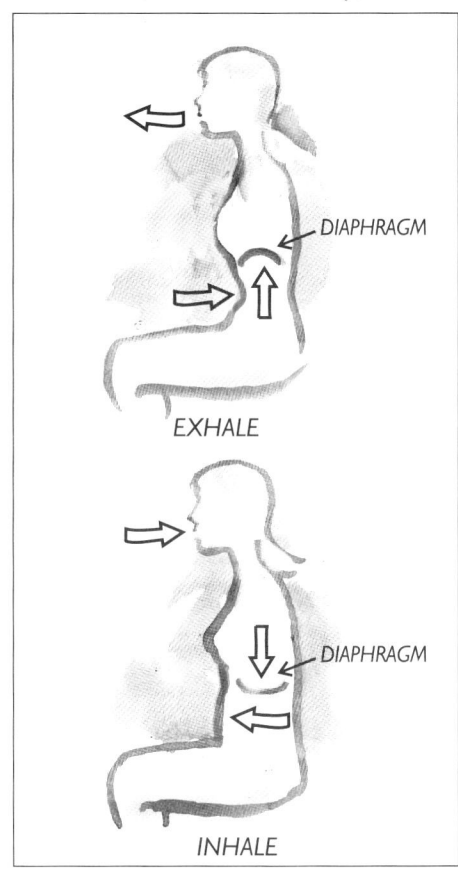

In abdominal breathing, two simultaneous events cause the diaphragm to move downward to form a flattened shape: 1) when we fill up our lungs with air, the diaphragm is compressed downward, and 2) we can control the movement of the diaphragm's muscles with our mind.

When the diaphragm flattens, it causes the stomach to expand. We can help the stomach along with a gentle nudging from our minds. The result of using the diaphragm and the stomach together is that, when inhaling, our lungs can extend to their maximum. This allows the air to reach the lungs' deepest recesses, the lower lobes, where the greatest number of veins are found to oxygenate the body. At the same time, the chest expands very little because the air fills our lungs in a downward and vertical manner and not in an outward or horizontal direction. The chest muscles remain relaxed. (Fig. A) When exhaling, the stomach contracts naturally as the diaphragm springs back to its rounded shape. (Fig. B) When the air leaves the lungs, it exits from the top part first with the lower lobes emptying last.

Deep abdominal breathing allows us to use the entire potential of our lungs. It is the most efficient, energizing, and calming way to promote good health and to sharpen our awareness. It grounds us into a clearer reality of who we are and where we fit in. When the breath goes deep, it allows us to "collect" ourselves, our inner strengths and feelings. At the same time, we connect with the universal life-force, the breath of life that contains the spirit of all living things.

5. Centering

Centering is a meditative process of seeking the middle point where mind and emotions find their natural harmony. It is a place of perfect balance. The image that comes to mind is that of a scale balancing two equal weights. Of course the workings of the mind and emotions are far more complex than a two-sided scale. However, when we "center," we do not consider the complexities of our feelings or thoughts but dive directly to the core of ourselves. That core is a place of peace and clarity from where the wisdom of The Middle Path springs.

I experience this center as both physical and something that is highly abstract. Physically I have a sense that my center is just below my bellybutton in the area of what the Chinese call "the tan t'ien." The tan t'ien is located approximately at the midpoint of the body. This sense of middle probably comes from many years of practicing T'ai Chi and Chi kung.

The center is also a place that is more than a physical point on the body's topography. When I meditate, I imagine my center to be a small dark abstract circle. I've discovered that upon reaching my center, I am able to see things clearly. My world changes or rather my take on the world is transformed. I can suddenly see the way I want myself to be. My perspective has broadened. Centering highlights my foibles and my goals in a way that I cannot ignore. Sometimes my center is filled by a shaved monk in black robes, sitting in meditation. The feeling he projects is one of great tranquillity and wisdom.

Once you find your center, you don't have to meditate to go there. You just have to tune it in. For example, the other day I was driving with my family to the beach. The children were getting rowdy in the back seat. I could feel my irritation building and I was heading for a blowup. I took a few deep breaths and tuned in my center. I felt the irritation transform to a course of action. I was able to tell them clearly and firmly that I wanted them to settle down. The entire process took a few seconds.

The work of centering is meant for practical use in daily life. Distractions, disturbances, and irritations are the tests that will try your soul. Yet they are the fodder against which you can gauge your progress. If something disturbs you, go to your center and try to stay there. If you lose it, come back again and again. Persevere! This is active meditation in the real world, wonderful training to reduce stress.

Recently I gave a talk to a support group of parents who were angry for various reasons and needed help in handling difficult situations. One woman told of her saga in trying to get medicine for her child from the health system. It was a catch 22 situation. She became very angry at the system and the bureaucrats who run it. I explained to her that by finding her center she could interact with the clerks who represent the system with clarity and purpose. The anger she displayed merely created an equal amount of resistance from them. I told her that what she wanted was the medicine and not the fight. If she had approached them from her center, she would have remained calm and flexible in her strategy. She agreed with me but she had no idea what her center is or how to find it. I suggested meditation to the group. We did a few exercises where I tried to show what I meant. However, I realized that the group would need the desire to learn the art of centering consistently before they could progress. Words are helpful but doing is far better.

I've found that the best way find the "center" is through purposeful and regular meditation. Usually, finding it does not happen instantaneously. It takes work. One of the best practices is the Standing Meditation of chapter VI. When standing, the body must find its central point of balance. It always moves slightly while adjusting its equilibrium, naturally finding its center. These small adjustments teach the mind to center subliminally. With time, the mind begins to mirror what the body does naturally. When the body and mind harmonize, the ground work is laid for entering the art of centering.

Another technique for centering is to close your eyes and breathe deeply. After you quiet your thoughts, try to visualize where your center is located. Then place your hands over that area and breathe into your hands. This is an excellent way to begin learning how to center.

6. Letting go

Once you find your center, it is far easier to let go of life's tribulations. If you habitually blame your boss or your children for feelings of being uptight, you will not be able to take control of your life. It is always easier to look for scapegoats outside yourself. It's him or her and not me that is the cause of my problems. The truth is that your response to outside irritants determines what kind of effect they will have on you. If you remove yourself from the problem and prefer not to deal with it, you are likely to discover that similar problems will crop up later. The face and the place may be different but the dilemma will be the same.

By centering and letting go, you can cope with the problems, sore points, and friction that arise from interacting with others. By letting go, you gain control in a way that allows you to be the captain of your destiny rather than a deck hand who takes orders. If you want to improve the quality of your life, you must realize that only you can do it. At the same time, be aware that the work of self-cultivation to become a better person ranks high on the chart of "life's worthy endeavors." It is a precious gift you have to give to family and friends – and to yourself.

As a way to underline the importance of each session of meditation, think of your effort in the following way: every time that you begin to practice one of the exercises in this book, you are training yourself to relax and let go in the real world. Think of yourself as an athlete in training, like a swimmer who is practicing a stroke outside the pool. Once you grasp the idea under easy conditions, then you can jump into deep waters and swim.

When you sit in a quiet room, focusing and breathing, you are preparing yourself to be calm and relaxed during the difficult times. You know, those moments when your kids are screaming at you or your wife (or husband) tells you to take out the garbage and, after a long day's work, all you want to do is sit and read the paper. You are training yourself not to blow up but to accept life's irritations with a calm and even temperament. You are learning to let go of the pettiness that narrows your thinking and shackles your imagination. This is the best kind of preparation for The Middle Path.

During your meditation sessions, strive to leave all your problems, worries, and external commitments at the door. Let them go! This is your time, your space, to do something special for yourself. It is not being selfish to take a temporary time-out to prepare yourself to be a healthier and better person. When you feel good and can think clearly, your contribution to your loved ones and to society will be greater.

Learning to let go through the various meditation and visualization techniques will whisk your mind on a temporary vacation from the cares and woes of the world.

After all, the root of the word "vacation," is to "vacate;" that is, in terms of meditation, to empty your mind, which in turn allows you to relax. These techniques will help you to rejoin your normal activities after a relatively short period feeling rejuvenated and refreshed.

When I speak of letting go and being more relaxed, I mean something different from spending an evening in front of the television or having a few drinks with friends. While this kind of leisurely activity can be pleasant, studies show that they do not adequately counteract the ill-effects of chronic stress. In fact sometimes being with friends or watching a gripping movie can make you more tense.

Before you can center and let go, you must limit your external input and focus your awareness. This results in the subsiding of the internal chatter. You begin to experience thoughts and feelings through the prism of ease rather than rigor, of being flexible rather than inflexible. You open up the closed parts of yourself.

Learning to let go requires the art of softening your countenance and easing the desire for control over others. The difference is nestled in the attitude of seeing a flower as a creation of color and beauty rather than as a thing to be cut and sold to customers. It is the fine line between love and lust, between a genuine sharing or exploiting your partner. It means developing healthy relationships of giving and taking, whether it be with another person or a creation of nature. It means not owning, changing or exploiting every person or thing in order to customize it for rapacious "wants." Letting go has a lot to do with accepting the other as something unique and valuable in its own right. Acceptance is the healing balm that neutralizes the obsession for control.

Similar to centering, letting go is something you can do during all your waking hours. It is an aspect of your meditation that you can bring into the real world, the practical world of human interaction. You need not compartmentalize the act of letting go by saying: "I'll let go of my pettiness during meditation but keep it the rest of the time." If you were to do that, you would lose much of meditation's benefits.

Keeping in mind these basic ingredients of letting go – along with the techniques of focusing the mind and calming it through abdominal breathing – you are well into your journey toward making the joys and benefits of meditation a reality. You will feel peaceful, a kind of external and internal relaxing of the mind, muscles, and joints. You will create an atmosphere where thoughts and feelings sharpen into focus while negative emotions, like anger and frustration, melt away. Letting go of your petulance and your resistances – those aspects of yourself that cage the "real" you – will allow you to feel vibrantly alive while reducing tension. Letting go frees your heart to love and to be loved.

Yet, a word of warning: you might feel none of these things. Sometimes, particularly in the beginning, one experiences only the stress of anger and frustration that has been building up in yourself for years. Your mind is like a swing, taut and knotted from being twisted around and around by the pressures of chronic stress. When released, it unravels with increasing speed until it straightens out. Then it begins to twist the other way. But eventually the manic swings of the mind will moderate and find a natural balance. The tension in your body/mind might cause you to experience some twisting flip-flops that sow doubts about your chosen practice, but this will pass. It took twenty or forty years to establish your patterns of tension and it will take awhile to refashion the way you wish to interact with the world.

Above all, be patient and kind to yourself. Do not put the same kind of demands on yourself to relax and to fulfill certain expectations in the same way you demanded success for yourself as a career person or a parent. It simply will not work. You will end up being the most "relaxed," uptight person on the face of the earth.

7. Visualization

Visualization is the use of the creative imagination during meditation. The meditator himself or an outside person guides the mind into the abstract experience of a directed fantasy. Despite the use of the word "fantasy," you should not think that the experience is unreal or has no effect on the body/mind. Visualization has a long and venerable history in the East, particularly in the meditation techniques of Taoism and Buddhism. It has also made strong inroads in the West. Research in Russia, for example, has demonstrated that athletes who spend time visualizing their peak performance do better than those who merely prepare themselves physically. Visualization is an important way in which the mind communicates with and directs the body.

The technique of visualization is more active than focusing. Focusing is generally not directed to a specific goal. It centers on self-observation or letting go.

With visualization, the meditator embarks on a specific agenda. Both visualization and focused meditation are valuable tools in the practice of stress reduction and improved health. They are ways to get in touch with and to make use of the Law of Transformation.

Over the last twenty years, visualization has gained increasing acceptance with the medical community and the public at large. While no one claims that it is a panacea, recent research demonstrates that visualization is an effective tool in helping many people cope with or cure their illnesses. Earlier we mentioned Dr. Simonton and others who have successfully used visualization in the treatment of cancer patients.

Visualization is also used to summon hidden images that lie dormant in the unconscious mind. This process reveals the character of the inner self and its fears. Finding one's own language of the unconscious can play an important role in healing the body/mind. These images can pinpoint specific problems and often suggest ways to resolve them.

Some people visualize mental images in their minds easily. They have a natural talent for it. Others find visualization very difficult. Yet the people who have difficulties need not be excluded from the practice of visualization. Visualization can take on other forms than abstract reflection. Many people have a natural inclination to experience feelings and emotions rather than the ability to create personal images. There are also people who are more intellectually oriented. Visualization is a multifaceted technique that can be shaped to the needs of each individual. If one kind of visualization does not work, try another. Generally everyone can find the type of visualization that works for him or her.

For example, imagine you have embarked on an exercise in which the facilitator asked you to visualize yourself as being well and happy. However, this image is not working for you. Play with the idea. Perhaps you could try to "sense" that your whole body feels good, as you relax the painful areas. A more intellectual approach is to search out your internal spirit guide (end of Chapter 3) and ask him or her what is wrong and how you might remedy the situation. You might try the smile meditation (Chapter 7).

Visualization can be done with all or just one of the senses. Some people visualize in color while others do so in black and white. Others might recall a funny incident that releases tension and allows them to relax. In visualization there is no right or wrong. Because of the variety of people's inclinations, the exercises taught in this book will explore many kinds of visualization techniques.

Some people believe that visualization is a kind of "lying" or "fooling" oneself. Visualization is a technique to help someone envision a "desired outcome," a method to guide the body/mind in the direction one wants to go. It is important to understand that visualization is *not* necessarily a reflection of what is happening in the moment! Visualization is similar to the archer when he aims his arrow. A bullseye is his "desired outcome." There is no deceit in taking aim.

In most cases we will not "fall" into good health or a more relaxed lifestyle in the same way one falls in love. We must seek it, will it, through effort and determination, and then have the good sense to let go at the right moment.

Summary

Before you begin the exercises in the following chapters, review the ideas that you have just read. You should be familiar enough with this chapter so that you will need to glance back only occasionally before you start your session.

Later, when you have achieved an ease and a familiarity with the concepts in this chapter, you can take a shortcut in the process of meditation by utilizing these three core concepts.

1. **Harmonize the body.** This means to focus on your posture, for example using the image of a string to draw your spine and head into alignment.
2. **Harmonize the breath.** Breathe abdominally.
3. **Harmonize the mind.** Quiet the mind and keep your attention in the present moment.

Be serious and diligent. A better quality of life is waiting for you. You need only choose it!

Chapter 5

Meditations and Visualizations

Concentrate on the goal of meditation

Do not listen with your ear

But listen with your mind;

Not with your mind

But with your breath.

Let the mind stop with your ear,

Let the mind stop with its images.

Breathing means to empty oneself....

Chuang Tzu

Introduction

This chapter will focus on the practical side of improving your health within the context of The Middle Path. You will learn a few simple yet extremely effective techniques of meditation and visualization. At this point, if you are familiar with "The Seven Steps of Meditation" in Chapter IV, you may continue. If not, take some time to review them. The ensuing exercises assume that you are familiar with the aforementioned basics of meditation.

Sitting Meditation

When practicing sitting meditation, there are many traditional ways to do it, such as the half-lotus or lotus position. The method of lotus sitting grew out of the Buddhist tradition. If you are familiar with these or other sitting positions, you may use them in your practice as long as you follow the instructions for proper posture, attitude and breath.

However, because of a knee problem, I find most Eastern ways of sitting uncomfortable and painful. I prefer to sit on a chair that provides my back with good support. The chair must be low enough that the feet rest comfortably on the floor. I do not recommend meditating in a soft easy chair that swivels or reclines backwards. The chair you choose should support you so you feel solid and upright. It should help you to keep your back vertical to the floor and ceiling.

1st Exercise:

Counting the Breaths

1. Cheng Man Ch'ing advised his students that their breathing should be "thin, long, quiet and slow...." Another Chinese sage recommended that when meditating, the breath should be so soft that it cannot be heard. This is the way, he advised, that the old can regain their youth. By traditional and modern accounts, being sensitive to how you breathe will have a positive bearing on the quality of the meditative experience.

2. Begin this exercise by breathing abdominally. As you breathe, count the breaths with your mind in this manner: 1 (inhale), 2 (exhale); 2 (inhale), 2 (exhale); 3 (inhale), 2 (exhale); 4 (inhale), 2 (exhale); 5 (inhale), 2 (exhale). Briefly, on the inhale you count from 1 to 10. The exhale *always* occurs on the count of 2.

3. In this exercise you do nothing more than focus on the breath and the counting of it. Keep track of how many times you get to ten without forgetting where you are in the count. This is a way of measuring your improvement. Often you will find that thought fragments or entire dialogues will interfere with your concentration. Gently bring your mind back to the breath and the count. This exercise can be deceptively simple.

4. In your initial sessions do not meditate over five minutes. As you become

more experienced in sitting quietly and maintaining your concentration on the breath, gradually increase the amount of time you spend on meditating until you reach twenty to thirty minutes.

5. You should practice this style of breathing and become proficient at it. Do not become discouraged. Counting the breath has the practical virtue of being a quick way to relax and focus. For this reason, we will use it as a warm-up for many of the techniques later on.

2nd Exercise:

Focusing

1. You have just practiced one kind of focusing where the breath becomes the object of your attention. Now you are ready to learn another method of focusing. Begin by counting your breaths for three sets of ten in the same manner as above. Here you are counting breaths as a warm-up.

2. When you feel relaxed and focused, shift your attention in a general way and allow your mind to be aware of how you are feeling. Observe what kinds of thoughts drift into your mind. This activity is a lot like people-watching, but here you are watching your own internal stream of consciousness. All you have to do is to remain objective and aware. Try not to judge whatever occurs as good or bad. It is what it is and nothing more.

Certain physical problems may appear. For example, you might feel aches in your back from sitting or your legs might become restless. Be sensitive to any feelings of pain as well as pleasure. Of course if the pain becomes unbearable, change your position. But don't forget to follow the instructions on proper posture.

3. Focusing provides you with the opportunity to experience what is going on inside your body/mind. Some of it may be nonsense. At the same time, there may be genuine insights into what is bothering you. Your subconscious mind may even hint at some possible solutions.

4. After a while, if you keep bringing your focus back to your meditation, you will discover that many of these distracting thoughts and sensations will subside. The process works something like this. If you throw a rock into a pond, it will create ripples that gradually dissipate outwards. The pond becomes calm again unless you

throw in another rock. Investing time and energy in your thoughts or sensations is the same as throwing another rock in the pond. You will generate more ripples, more thoughts. Remaining an objective observer allows the ripples to float away without leaving a lasting impression. The mind, like the pond, grows tranquil.

5. One technique that I've found particularly useful in quieting my mind is to invite my thoughts in as a welcomed friend. Instead of ignoring them, I try to honor their legitimacy without embracing them. They are, after all, parts of me. They may represent my role as father, neighbor, community figure. They may represent anger, jealousy, obligations, or love. By acknowledging them and their rightful place in my world, they lose their power to disturb my meditation. At the moment they are visitors who must wait until I have finished with the task at hand.

6. When you become proficient in the art of focusing, your mind will develop a calm and centered detachment. It will help you to clearly distinguish between important and unimportant matters. You will be less easily sidetracked in your goals. A focused mind will make a dramatic difference in your efforts to reduce stress as well as to achieve an inner clarity.

3rd Exercise:

Using the Mind's Eye to Relax the Body

The following exercise combines the techniques of deep breathing, focusing and visualization in order to relax the entire body. What is unique about this technique is that you will learn how to direct your attention throughout the body in order to achieve complete relaxation. When you become an expert in deep relaxation techniques like this one, you can call on their benefits practically anywhere; in the office, driving your car or standing in line at the bank.

One of my Chinese teachers of meditation explained to me that I must learn to see with "dual-vision." He meant that it is possible to peer inside my body just as easily as I see outwardly into the world. The "mind's eye," which is the tool of this inner vision, can be trained to do this. Chinese meditators believe that they can visualize and direct the healing power of their internal energy (ch'i) through specific pathways in the body called meridians. Many Western healers and meditators make similar claims of being able to see the color and texture of people's auras.

Whether the meditator of the mind's eye is from the East or the West, he or she is utilizing the Law of Transformation: **Consciousness>Energy>Material World.** The mind's eye is one of many techniques to focus and change consciousness. It is a marriage of passive meditation techniques with an active and focused imagination.

Everyone has the ability to see with the mind's eye. Yet most people do not use this gift because they are unaware of its existence.

Using the mind's eye is something like having an intuitive sense about things. Most of us have used our intuition at one time or another. For example, you might have had a "feeling" that your boss would support your proposal or you "knew" that your sport's team would win. These kinds of intuitions spring up spontaneously and often hit the mark. While most people pay little attention to these hunches, there are a select few who make an art of summoning this kind of natural prophecy.

In a similar way, your body may signal the mind with certain intuitions about what is going on internally. There may have been times when you "sensed" that you were going to be sick before the development of the physical symptoms. Perhaps the mind's seeing is an intuitive reflection of the body's cry for help.

There are two important roles that the mind can assume in relation to the body. The mind can be a diagnostician and a healer. By consciously cultivating the natural bonding of the body/mind, we can employ the mind's eye as a tool to search out problems as though it were our own private CAT scan. Equally important, through innovative techniques of visualization, the mind's eye can become a tool for healing. In the next exercise the mind will learn to reconnoiter and to relax our stressed-out bodies.

But how does one teach another person to use such an intangible tool as the mind's eye? As I wrote this chapter, I was helping my five year old daughter learn how to ride her two-wheel bike. My role was more that of a facilitator than that of a teacher. My main task was to run alongside of her to make sure that she did not injure herself when she lost her balance and fell. I reminded her to shift her weight in order to keep her balance and to guide the bike in the center of the lane. Gradually she began to get the hang of it. She maintained her balance a little better each time. After a while she realized that she was getting it. She said to me, "How come my body can suddenly do it?" I wanted to answer her with a clear explanation, but I found it difficult to give lucid reasons for such an internal experience. The best I could do on the spot was: "Your body just does it."

If you have experienced something like this before, then you know exactly what I mean. Developing balance on a bike has something to do with internal sensitivity and adjustment. My daughter had to be sensitive to just how much weight she needed in order to maintain her balance. What's more, it required a "delicate" sensitivity. Too much of a weight shift in either direction would cause a crash.

All of the above applies to learning how to engage the mind's eye. You simply have to do it, use it, work with it, hone it, until directing the mind's eye is as familiar as riding a bicycle. Your mind's eye is waiting to do your bidding, but it may be asleep from years of neglect. Once you master its intricacies, like riding a bike, you will never forget how. The following exercise is designed for beginners. Take your time, be patient, and practice until you feel comfortable with the exercise.

1. Preparation:

Before using the mind's eye, it is important to empty out and to begin with a clean slate. Take your usual sitting position and do three sets of focused abdominal breathing where you count to ten. Feel your body/mind sink into a relaxed state. If you do not feel relaxed, take your time and breathe some more. As you continue to breathe deeply, observe the state of your mind – its thoughts and feelings. Be an objective observer. After a period of time, you may be able to skip most or all of the preparation and jump right into this exercise. But don't take shortcuts until you've mastered the art of bringing yourself to ground zero, that is, emptying out your mind.

2. Feet:

Focus the attention of your mind's eye on your toes. If you have a problem "seeing" your toes, wiggle them. Focus your mind on their movement. Then, with the out-breath, relax them. You do not have to actually "see" your toes in your mind's eye in order to relax them. Feeling them may be enough.

Next shift your attention to the bottoms of your feet, first the arch and then the heel. Be certain they are resting comfortably on the floor and, with the breath, relax them. Try to visualize breathing into the places you want to relax.

3. Ankle, Knee and Hip Joints:

Shift the focus of your mind's eye to your ankles. Relax them by opening and softening them. Breathe into them. When they feel relaxed, move your attention to your calves. Shake them a bit to guide the mind's eye to the exact location. Relax your calves. If this causes some tension, take a time-out and focus on your breath. Then return to the calves.

Next, focus the mind's eye on the knees. Follow the same procedures that you applied to the ankles.

Relax your knees! Breathe deeply into them. As you breathe through the nose, visualize the air being inhaled through the knees. It is something like breathing through the pores of your skin.

Move on to your thighs. Relax them. Let them sink into the chair and feel heavy. Breathe into them.

Gradually shift your attention to the hip joints. Relax and breathe into them. Take a few moments to familiarize yourself with the hip joints. When sitting, they form a large crease where the legs fit into the joints. Gently run your fingers along them. By relaxing and loosening these joints, your body will move more freely and gracefully.

Pause for a few moments. With your mind's eye, review what you have done by scanning your legs from the tips of your toes to your hip joints.

Many people find that relaxing their legs is a turning point in relaxing the entire body because tension often congregates in the legs.

4. Genitals, Crotch and Buttocks:

Shift your mind's eye to your genitals. Relax them. Breathe into them. If you begin to have any sense of sexual arousal, simply go to the next body part. Sexual arousal will cause you to lose your focus and the benefits of this meditation.

Now focus on the crotch area. Relax and breathe into it. To help the mind's eye focus on this area, gently squeeze the crotch and the buttocks together a few times. This will bring your attention there.

Feel your buttocks sitting firmly on the chair. Let them sink into the chair. They should feel heavy. Check to see if the anus is open. If not, open and relax it. Once again, breathe into the buttocks and crotch. Relax.

5. The Back:

Now, take a moment to check your posture. Because your attention has been elsewhere, you may be slouching against the back of the chair. Realign yourself. Use the image of the string gently drawing your head upwards. This delicate sense of balanced counterpoise is extremely healthy for the spine because it gently separates any vertebrae that might be collapsing on their neighbor. It also opens up the circuitry of the spine and allows the messages of the body/mind to flow freely.

At this point we are going to relax the back in three sections: *lower* (from the coccyx or tailbone to the top of the hip bone), *middle* (from the top of the hip bone until the lower part of the shoulder blade), and *upper* (from the shoulder blades to the shoulders).

Shift your attention to the lower back. Use your mind's eye to relax and breathe into this area. Imagine that as the head is being gently pulled upwards by a string, the lower back is sinking down and relaxing. This creates the subtle perception that the spine is lengthening by small increments. Continue to breathe into the lower back.

Now, move up the spine to the middle back. Try to visualize the vertebrae along the spine. Relax and gently straighten them with your mind's eye. Tuck the chin in a bit and gently stretch the head up. Keep the image of the suspended head in mind. Then relax the middle back on both sides of the spine. Let the muscles sink down with an easy sense of restfulness. Give them a respite from holding up the back all day by allowing the head and string to do the work.

Continue your ascent along the spine to the shoulder blades. Each time you breathe out, let the shoulders sink down, allowing the upper back to relax. Simultaneously, the back of the neck and the head are lengthening. We are consciously experiencing our back muscles sinking while the spine is being gently pulled in opposite directions. (Refer to figure, p. 58)

Another useful image is to think of your body as a suit of clothes suspended from a hanger. The head, neck and spine represent the hanger and are holding things in place. This allows the rest of the body, particularly the muscles, to relax completely. At the same time the all-important energy paths of the spine open in the same way that water flows freely through a hose when the kinks are removed.

Now, review the entire back to be certain that it remains relaxed.

6. The Back of the Neck:

Shift your attention to the back of the neck and relax it. Roll your head on your neck if you need to help the mind's focus. Think "up," but do not force the neck to lengthen. Along with imagining a string, by simply suggesting to the neck the notion of 'up,' you will subtly initiate a gentle realignment that will occur over time.

Try to relax the neck and breathe into it. Find the point where the head balances naturally on the neck and where you feel the least amount of stress on the muscles. The more you bring your body into balance with proper alignment, the less strain there will be on the muscles and the less tension you will experience.

Continue to relax and breathe until you are ready to go on.

7. The Head:

Focus the mind's eye on the top of the head. I often imagine a picture that contains the shape of my brain within my skull. I try to relax and breathe while keeping that image in mind. Sometimes I imagine that my brain is suffused with a rich golden light.

Next, shift your attention to the sides of your head, the area between your ears and your eyes, a common headache zone. Take some time to focus there and simply breathe and relax. Then move your attention to the forehead. If you breathe and relax the area, the wrinkles will disappear. Gradually shift your focus to the eyes. Be sure that they are gently closed. Breathe into them. When you gently squeeze them, you might feel more waves of relaxation roll over your eyes and perhaps your face.

Now, take a moment to focus on the breath. Feel the air flowing in and out your nostrils. Be sure that you are breathing abdominally. Take your time and move on only when you feel ready.

The next stop is the jaws. People often hold the jaws in a clenched position, which may cause headaches. Let them drop down slightly to relax with the breath. If you feel tension in your jaws, breathe into them several times until they release.

Then shift your attention to the mouth. Gently close it. Breathe deeply and relax the lips.

With your mind's eye, review the neck, head and face. Be certain that everything you have relaxed has remained so.

8. Throat, Chest and Stomach:

There is a special imagery from Chinese meditation techniques that you may want to use here. With your mouth, gather your saliva on your tongue. Then with your mind's eye, imagine that the saliva in your mouth is the shape of a golden pearl. (If you do not have enough saliva, place your tongue on the roof of your mouth. This usually produces saliva). Swallow the golden pearl. Watch as it descends through your throat to your stomach, spreading its glow and a warm sense of healing energy. Try to visualize your throat, esophagus and stomach as being suffused with golden light.

If you cannot do this visualization or feel uncomfortable with it, wait until you become more experienced in using your mind's eye. Often ideas in visualization will not work well the first time.

Next, fill your lungs with air through deep abdominal breathing. If you feel ready, imagine the air that you breathe in is golden like rich sunlight. When it touches your lungs, they also become golden. Continue to focus on relaxing the entire chest through deep breathing.

Shift your focus down to the area of the stomach, a distance spanning from the solar plexus to the pubic hairline. Pay attention to how the stomach expands and contracts with each breath. Try to smooth out its movements so that the rhythm is deep, slow, and without tension, that it flows in and out like waves lapping against the shore. With your mind's eye, tell your stomach to relax. This happens more easily when exhaling as the diaphragm softens and returns to its normal size.

The key is: **relax, relax, relax!**

Before you go on, check your posture. Be certain that you have not relaxed yourself out of the proper alignment.

9. Shoulders, Elbows, Wrists and Hands:

Move your attention to the shoulders where the arms fit into the joints. Simply breathe and relax. Slowly bring your gaze to the muscles between the shoulders and the elbows. Continue to focus and breathe into the muscles. With each exhale let them relax a little more. Turn your attention to the elbows. Move them a bit to help you to focus the mind's eye on them. Breathe and relax into them.

Imagine that your elbows have a valve in them that you can open to allow your body's energy to flow freely through.

Then feel your forearms resting on your legs. Let them relax totally in a downward direction like the limbs of a raggedy-anne doll. Allow them to sink into your thighs. They should feel heavy and completely relaxed. Breathe into them as you focus on the wrists. Let them relax completely on your thighs, so that they feel heavy and even lethargic. (They may feel inflated or bloated. This is nothing to worry about. It will pass.)

Next, turn your attention to the hands. Like the wrists, let them completely relax on the thighs. Have a sense of them being heavy. Imagine that with each inhale and exhale, you are breathing through the tips of your fingers and into the hands, wrists and arms.

10) The Entire Body

Now, as you breathe deeply, visualize a picture of your entire body being suffused in the healing balm of golden energy. Begin from your stomach and move downwards and upwards simultaneously as though the light were a river overflowing its banks. With one grand sweep of your mind's eye, visualize your entire body awash in golden light, from the top of your head to the bottoms of your feet. Stay with this image as long as it feels comfortable.

If you managed successfully with most of this meditation, you have come a long way on the road to better health and stress reduction. Most importantly, be consistent. Practice this meditation at least once a day.

Helpful Hints:

1) This meditation was not written down in tablets of stone. You should feel free about experimenting with it. If some of the visualizations do not suit you, turn your attention to other forms of visual imagery. Moreover, the above meditation will operate effectively as a method to improve health and reduce stress without the visual imagery. If you do only the basics, that is, focusing, relaxing and breathing with certain body parts in mind, you will relax your body and experience a reduction in stress. This is a powerful exercise. If the color gold suggested here does not feel right, try other colors like a whitish gold, green or blue. These are also healing

colors. Do what feels right for you. The above meditation is merely a guide and a structure to get you started.

    2) The meditations presented in this book have worked successfully for me and my students. From past experience, however, there is seldom universal agreement among people whom I have guided as to efficacy of a particular exercise. We all have different talents, tastes and inclinations.

    2) Practice the above exercise when you have at least twenty minutes during one of your regular meditation sessions. You should practice it until it becomes natural in the same way that riding a bicycle becomes second nature. Make a tape of this exercise, either using your voice or the voice of a friend, or purchase the cassette that goes with this book. Speak slowly and clearly. Pause after each body part in order to give yourself plenty of time to breathe and relax. It is important not to feel hurried.

    3) When you become fluent in this meditation technique, you can take some shortcuts. One of these shortcuts is called "scanning." Let's say that you are on a bus and you want to relax. Close your eyes and watch your breathing for ten counts. Then, as you continue to breathe deeply, the mind's eye quickly surveys your body beginning with the toes. You can do this in a few minutes or less. After a while you can scan your body in a few seconds, although it is more effective when you take more time. You can also scan only those parts of the body that feel tense. Another possibility is that you can scan only those areas that you know are keys in relaxing the entire body.

    Personally, I have discovered that, by merely closing my eyes and slightly exerting pressure with my eyelids, waves of relaxation wash over my eyes, forehead and upper skull. You will find your own keys to relaxation.

    4) Another shortcut is to focus the mind's eye on one part of the body. For example, after preparing yourself to meditate, focus on the right hand only. By completely relaxing it in the manner we learned in the above meditation, you can relax the entire body. A more advanced level of this technique is learning to raise the temperature of the hand. Recent research demonstrates that this change of temperature can reduce and in some cases eliminate migraine headaches. Using similar meditative techniques, highly trained yogis dressed only in a loin cloth can meditate out-of-doors in the middle of winter and melt the snow around them.

5) As a general rule, if you encounter a place in your body that makes you feel uncomfortable or nervous during meditation, pay attention to this important signal. It may be a place that is generating tension for the entire body. By devoting special attention to relaxing this tense spot, you may discover that the rest of the body will slip into a state of deep repose.

6) When you become an expert, your mind's eye can go inside the anatomical parts of the body and relax each individual joint. I've found it helpful to study a map of the body's anatomical structure. This gave me a clear image of the inner body to work with.

The Importance of Doing Less:

We have discussed several valuable techniques and methods of meditation in this chapter. Now I want to do an about-face. I want to give you permission to do *almost* nothing at all. To say it better, you can do nothing at all within the context of a simple and relaxed structure. With all the demands on your life, this chapter of meditative techniques might seem like just another obligation that you *have to do* and, if you do not do it, you will suffer the consequences. The result of such pressure is that this book will accomplish the opposite of what was intended: it will add more stress to your already stressful life instead of lessening it.

"Doing less" represents a way of balancing the obsession of always needing to do something to feel complete. We often try to do so much that we accomplish very little. We are similar to the proverbial chicken that runs around in circles with its head cut off. The truth is that you are already complete, and all the strivings to do something (like the exercises in this book) are only road maps to help you find the way back home.

Doing less is also a way to neutralize the powerful dictates of our superegos. In China, over two thousand years ago, Confucianism became the official state religion with strict rules for behavior in society. To balance the Confucian limitations on individual prerogatives, some philosophers, specifically those connected to Taoism, delighted in tweaking the nose of the official orthodoxy. Chuang Tzu was one of those wise thinkers. This is one of his aphorisms: "Once the fish is caught, the trap can be thrown away." Once you grasp the principle of something, you don't need to think about it anymore because you have internalized its essence.

In language, grammar is a good example of throwing away the trap once one knows how to speak or write. A good writer or speaker has little if any need for a grammar book. Similarly, doing less allows you to toss away the external trappings of life once you have grasped the structure of, say, how to meditate. It also allows you to focus on the elusive sense of your true self instead of being excessively self-conscious. This is another important context to understand the virtue of doing less and achieving more, which is an important aspect of following The Middle Path.

The Virtue of Uselessness

A corollary of doing less is the virtue of uselessness. Chuang Tzu told the following story.

A sage was walking along the road with his disciples. It was a hot day and he saw a large tree that provided enough shade so that all of them could rest under it. As they sat enjoying a respite from the hot rays of the sun, the sage explained that this tree was a living example of the virtue of uselessness. Because its limbs were gnarled and full of knots, no carpenter could use its wood for building. As a result, while the woodcutters felled the other trees around it, this useless tree remained standing. It continued to grow, providing shade for weary travelers.

The tree is a metaphor for meditators. Sometimes, by meditating and, in the eyes of many, being useless, a person can change his or her perspective on life. Similarly, that person's knowledge and understanding can provide shade for travelers who are sweltering in the heat of life's difficult moments.

Summary

Students have asked me this question: with so many things to think about such as breath, posture and visualization, how is it possible to combine them in an effective practice? The answer is that you should do what you can and not overdo. Do not bite off more than you can chew. Strive for a little progress each day rather than trying to grasp it all in one sitting.

Bear in mind that you are developing a skill. You must be aware of and sensitive to each step of that process. Becoming proficient in the techniques of meditation is something like learning to drive a car with a stick shift. A beginner must learn to manipulate the gas, clutch, and gear shift while simultaneously concentrating on the road. This may seem like a daunting task that you will never accomplish. In time the beginner discovers that there is a delicate point of contact where the clutch engages the drive shaft and, at that moment, just the right amount of pressure must be applied to the gas pedal. With patience, determination and practice, the driver begins to move the car down the road, at first jerkily and at last, as smooth as if driving an automatic shift.

Meditation requires great sensitivity in order to achieve the integration of body, breath and mind. Fortunately, it is a skill that you can learn. If you will be patient, determined and follow the ways of The Middle Path, you will succeed in your meditative practices. You will come to understand what Suzuki Roshi meant: you will experience nothing special and, at the same time, it will be something quite extraordinary.

Chapter 6

Standing Meditation:
Rooting the Body, Balancing the Mind

The superior man achieves harmony

In his character and conduct.

He does not waver.

How steadfast is his strength!

He stands in the middle position,

And does not lean to one side or the other.

Confucius

Introduction

My first encounter with Standing Meditation occurred one morning when I had brought my daughters to a children's park to play. In the park, there was a group of students and their teacher practicing T'ai Chi. Off to the side, under the shade of a large oak tree, was an elderly Chinese man. With his eyes closed and knees slightly bend, he stood quietly in meditation. His arms were stretched toward the tree's trunk as if embracing it. I recall watching his body gently swaying back and forth. Despite his age, his face bore no sign of wrinkles. In my mind, he epitomized serenity and rootedness. He seemed totally at one with the tree.

Later I read why one Chinese master of Standing Meditation preferred this practice. "When standing," he said, "the organs move, when doing other kinds of exercises, the body moves." While perhaps exaggerating, his view encapsulates the strong emphasis that many Chinese teachers place on internal work to strengthen the body and to calm the mind. There is an important idea in Chinese thought that in stillness there is movement (the internal organs) and in movement there is stillness.

Standing meditation is a complete exercise that brings about total body/mind involvement. It balances the body's internal energies and calms the mind's thoughts and emotions. It is easy to learn, easy to do and represents a perfect example of how doing less can become more, the way of The Middle Path. I teach "standing" in all my classes and I try to stand at least once every day, preferably in the morning.

Standing meditation is very popular in China. These adepts of stillness prefer to stand in parks or along river banks with their eyes closed, inhaling the early morning air and merging with the healthy vibrations of the natural environment around them. The Chinese name for it is Zhan Zhuang (pronounced "jan jong") which means "standing foundation." Often it is translated, "standing like a tree." Not surprisingly, enthusiasts of standing meditation like to practice in close proximity to a tree.

In standing meditation, the image of a tree is both powerful and appropriate. Trees have roots that sink deep into the ground. To survive, trees must be rooted and yet flexible when strong winds blow. People must acquire the same attributes to survive life's tornadoes. Standing meditation helps the practitioner to become "rooted" or "grounded" in his or her life. At the same time, the body's limbs remain soft and supple. The mind must also be flexible in times of trouble so it can find the path of survival.

Being "grounded" is crucial if one wishes to lead a healthy lifestyle. People who are not "grounded" or whose grounding is weak tend to be spacey. They are disconnected from reality and are often unable to establish a clear direction for their lives.

I often see this lack of grounding in beginning T'ai Chi students. These students tend to create unstable and misshapen postural stances when learning the T'ai Chi form. Once they strengthen their grounding with a balanced stance, they move more gracefully and with more focus. Grounding allows them to become an efficient and vibrant vehicle for whatever their goals might be, whether to take a proper stance in T'ai Chi, to develop a stable relationship with a mate, or to pursue a successful avocation.

When this grounding occurs, it flows into the other facets of one's life. How does this work? If you paint one wall of your house, you will probably need to paint the others because the clean wall will highlight the unpainted ones. Similarly, a change in one area of your life will influence the total picture. Becoming more grounded and simultaneously more relaxed will bring about positive changes, sometimes so subtle that you might not notice it until much later.

Trees are also our friends. They nourish us. They give us shade from the sun and food for our bodies. They filter the air for all living things on the planet. Trees also teach us humility. Their largeness is an awesome reminder that life abounds on this planet with a majesty that outshines even the size of the human ego. Through standing meditation, it is possible to develop a profound connection to trees and to nature. It is even possible to feel gratitude and to express it in the silence of mutual communion. Martin Buber called this wondrous moment, "I-Thou" in contrast to the impersonal "I-It."

Standing meditation is best practiced in nature where you are close to trees and flowers. Your backyard will do fine. A park is also suitable if you can find a quiet corner. It is preferable to stand in the shade of a tree. However, if the sun does not bother you or if it is a cold day, you may stand in the sun but with your back to it. Do not practice this form of meditation in the bitter cold, in the rain, or in a strong wind. If you are indoors, choose a quiet room that is well ventilated with soft lighting. As a beginner, practice for only a few minutes. Gradually increase your time to at least twenty minutes. It will be time well spent.

Preparation:

Find a flat spot where the ground is neither bumpy nor sloping. It is better not to do standing meditation on concrete if you can help it. Place your feet shoulder-width apart, parallel and toes on the same line. The knees should be slightly bent and unlocked. Straighten the back with the head lifting upwards as though being gently drawn towards the heavens with a string. Try to imagine that the string is doing the work of aligning the body. Allow the spine to fall naturally downward like a string of pearls. Tuck the chin slightly inward. The head should be upright and flat so that you could balance a book on top of it. The eyes can be closed or half-open. Relax the shoulders, chest and stomach downwards. Relax the buttocks and open the anus. Your arms should hang comfortably at your side. The elbows are slightly bent while the hands are parallel to the front of the body. The fingers are straight but not stiff and spread as though little balls were placed between them in the webbing. This is the first posture.

Now you are ready to begin. Breathe deeply with abdominal breathing. Stand and allow your mind to relax. In the beginning it might help to focus on counting your breath. Then let go of this. Allow your thoughts to come and go until they settle down. The goal is to relax and to be with yourself completely in the present moment. As you progress, you may feel a kind of internal and external balance that produces a state of well-being.

1st Posture

Do not stand like a statue but allow your body to gently sway and to find its natural equilibrium. This is in line with the idea of "centering". When your body finds its center, it will help your mind to do the same.

Your legs may begin to ache or feel restless after a while. This is normal. Your leg muscles will need some time to become accustomed to this kind of standing. Occasionally your legs may shake a bit. This is also not unusual. The Chinese believe that this is a sign that blockages are being opened and the Ch'i is beginning to flow unfettered. Sometimes you may feel sore in your back or some other place. This is often a warning of an area that is holding tension. Try to relax the sore points with your mind. But do not push yourself to the point where you grow to dislike this exercise. Do a reasonable amount each day and gradually try to increase it. *Do not overdo or be an overachiever.* We are doing these moderate exercises with an eye to the long run. A little progress each day is far better than a quick burn-out.

2nd Posture

After a few minutes, you can change to the

3rd Posture

second posture (previous page) of *"Embracing the Tree."* Imagine that you are holding a large beach ball against your chest to get the right form. Once that is achieved, it is important to focus on the idea of embracing the trunk of a tree and becoming solid and grounded like a tree.

When your arms grow tired, you can hold the ball from the bottom, the third posture, or return to the original Standing Meditation position. Whatever postures you decide to do, you should finish your meditation with the first posture.

There are other postures in traditional Standing Meditation. However, in keeping with The Middle Path, the exercises in this book strive for simplicity in learning and in practice. Just as doing is often better than words, doing less is better than doing too much.

Visualization:

The goal of this visualization is two-fold: to connect you to the earth and to increase your energy level. This meditation can be done while sitting but I prefer to do it standing, out-of-doors and next to a tree. Try it both ways and determine what works best for you. Above all, be pragmatic!

Begin by taking the Standing Meditation pose. Prepare yourself for the meditation by doing three sets of abdominal breathing. Relax and focus.

When you are ready, imagine that there is a small ball of golden light in your lower belly, about two to three inches below your belly-button. (The Chinese call this place the "tan t'ien", and sometimes translate it as "the ocean of breath"). With each inhale, visualize that the ball is growing larger until it fills your entire stomach area. You might want to use this imagery: each breath is like a bellows blowing on and increasing the size and intensity of the golden ball.

With your mind's eye and with the breath, guide the light from the ball in your stomach to your hip joints and gently send it down the thighs. Let the golden light continue downwards through the knees into the calves and ankles and finally reaching your feet. Stop for a moment and scan your legs to your belly. Make sure the light runs in a continuous line. Breathe and relax.

Next, imagine that the golden light is sinking into the earth from the bottoms of your feet (a point called the "Bubbling-Well Spring" by the Chinese). This light begins to burrow into the ground like the roots of a tree splitting off into separate sheaths of golden light. Guide these roots of light deeper and deeper into the earth until they reach the earth's molten center that is the same color as your golden light. Then let the light of your body and the light at the center of the earth merge and become one. Feel this connection and try to see it clearly. Breathe and relax.

Now, with your mind's eye, gradually bring the earth's golden light into your roots and guide it upwards. It may flow naturally on its own. When it reaches the soles of your feet, let the light continue into your feet and fill your toes, arches and heels. This powerful and yet soothing light continues upwards, spreading through your calves, knees and thighs, filling your hips and flowing into your stomach. Scan this river of golden light from your stomach until the earth's molten core and back again. Make sure it is one continuous stream. Breathe and relax.

In a general way, guide the light throughout your body. Let its golden aura spread like a soft cloud expanding in the sky. When it reaches the top of your head, send your mind's eye into the heavens above and bring down the golden light of the sun. (This is particularly effective if done out-of-doors.) At a point on the top of your head where there is a slight indentation, the sun's light and the light inside your body, which is connected to the light from the center of the earth, merge like the confluence of two rivers of pure energy.

You are the conduit, the vessel, that contains this primal energy. You are connected to the sky above and the earth below. Your body/mind is the meeting-point where the heavenly and earthly energies are harmonized and integrated, where angel and animal become one. Simply breathe, relax and let the energy balance naturally. Hold this imagery in your mind's eye until you feel it is time to end the meditation.

Continue to relax and breathe. Let go entirely of the light imagery. Return your focus to your breath. Feel your feet solidly standing on the ground. Listen to the sounds of the world around you, the birds singing or the wind whispering through the trees. Have a sense of your physical body being a solid part of the material world, that you are special and you belong here. When you feel ready, open your eyes and gradually return to your normal daily routines.

Special Needs

Standing Meditation is one of the easiest exercises to modify for people with "special needs." If you cannot stand, then do it sitting. Keep the image of the tree in mind. This is a key component in Standing Meditation. Find a bench near a tree. Instead of sending the light through the bottoms of your feet, you may want to send it out from your spine, the area of the coccyx.

In my special needs classes, some students stand for as long as they can and then they finish the exercise sitting down.

For people with weak legs, Standing Meditation strengthens them. The Chinese say that illness comes through the legs. If the legs are strong, then one can exercise and envigorate the immune system. Don't give up too easily and, remember: **don't overdo!**

Summary

Standing Meditation is particularly beneficial in the morning. I find that it helps to clear the cobwebs from my mind after a night's sleep. Over time, if you practice regularly, you will discover that you will feel more relaxed and balanced. You will also develop a deep sense of being grounded, that is, of feeling strongly connected to the ways of the world and yet sublimely detached from many worldly cares that previously troubled you. Standing Meditation is one of the best techniques for integrating and harmonizing all aspects of the body/mind.

Chapter 7

Help for the Soul

Everyone should know that
You can't live in any other way
Than by cultivating the soul.

Apuleius, Roman writer

The Forgiveness Meditation

True forgiveness is merciful and frees the soul to love. Finding the capacity to forgive and being able to ask for forgiveness can help set us right again. No matter how much knowledge we have or how many techniques to reduce stress we learn, they will be meaningless unless we walk the two-way street of reconciliation, with ourselves and with others. Forgiveness is the ultimate "letting go."

We must first forgive ourselves for straying from ourselves. Then, if we are to be forgiven for our mistakes, we must also reach deep inside and forgive those who have wounded us. Anger against others is a heavy burden to shoulder day in and day out. Holding on to grudges is a sure-fire way to ensure that our hearts will remain closed. If we cannot ask forgiveness or forgive, how can we expect the same in return? Dag Hammarskjöld observed: "We can only believe this is possible (to be forgiven) if we ourselves can forgive."

True atonement is the music of health. It is a scale of harmony that implies a balance of tones (words, thoughts, and feelings). Atonement can also be understood as the miracle of "at-one-ment" where the broken or tarnished relationship to one's own psyche, to family, to community, to the physical environment, and ultimately to God is restored. The physical immortality of the Eden may be beyond our reach, but living a full and rich life is still available to us. It is close to us because it dwells within us. We may always suffer some degree of dis-ease. That goes with the turf of being human. Nevertheless, by re-connecting to our own unique inner vision, a path that requires absolute honesty and integrity, we embark on the journey of becoming whole again.

In Judaism there is an important idea called "tikkun haolam." It means to "repair or to fix the world." Tikkun haolam conveys the sense of putting things right and, by doing so, promoting harmony in the world. True forgiveness is a God-given tool to restore the shattered harmony between man and man (woman and woman) and the entire creation. But "tikkun haolam" is more than a patch job to stop the roof from leaking. It means to start over again, a ripping down of the old and a building of the new. It is a radical rejection of historical necessity because forgiveness has the ability to turn the clock back to zero and to begin anew.

Sometimes you can ask for forgiveness on a one-to-one basis. The Forgiveness Meditation mentally prepares you to do this. However, often you cannot forgive someone personally because he or she is not available due to death or that person's whereabouts is unknown. In the latter two examples this meditation may prove especially helpful.

You may find the Forgiveness Meditation very emotional. Tears may flow. Just be in the present with what you are feeling. By unlocking deep emotions you are beginning to free yourself from their burden, which is often reflected in body/mind disease. The well-known author Marianne Williamson wrote: "Atonement is so gentle you need but whisper to it and all its power will rush to your assistance and support."

If the person also wronged you, have some compassion for his or her faults. You can also be compassionate with yourself. Forgive yourself for having made a mistake. Keep in mind that it takes two to tangle. Accentuate the positive in others and yourself. In the Moslem tradition, there is an interesting story about Jesus that illustrates this idea of a positive outlook:

> *Jesus and the disciples came upon the carcass of a dog.*
> *The disciples said: "What a stench it makes!"*
> *Jesus answered: "How white are its teeth!"*

When you are forgiving and compassionate to others, you will discover that this feeling carries over into your daily life. Forgiveness and compassion open the heart to more loving and healthy relationships. There is nothing more damaging to health than the stress of feeling lonely and isolated, which is often the result of shouldering painful grudges. The Forgiveness Meditation provides us with one way to reach out to others through an act of contrition.

If, at the end of this meditation, you do not feel complete, then return to the meditation and try to discover what is holding things back. Do it from your heart and not from anger. You'll know when it comes from your heart. You may feel like crying because the hurt becomes a tear. And if there is still no closure, end the meditation but come back to it on another day. Keep trying. One day there will be a breakthrough.

Begin the Forgiveness Meditation with the correct posture, breath and focusing. Breathe adominally for at least thirty times. Relax your body and empty your mind. Take your time. Right preparation is crucial.

When you are ready, visualize the person you want to forgive or to ask forgiveness from. Review the events that led to the problem between the two of you. Be absolutely clear about what happened. How did the wrongs occur? Then, give up the rights and wrongs. Watch them fly out the window or flush them down the toilet. With all your heart and soul, ask for his or her forgiveness. Or, you do the forgiving! Do so in simple, straight-forward language. Don't beat around the bush. Embrace the person with your heart and let there be love between you. Fill each other up with the warmth of forgiveness. Remember, you have the power to repair a hole in the world by opening your heart and forgiving.

Now, be absolutely clear: the matter is over and done with from now and forever more!

Coping With Fear and Anxiety

Before the publication of this book, I explained to my mother some of its basic ideas. "If you are teaching people how to relax," she said, "why not help those who are suffering from fear." At the time my mother had recently been operated on for cancer. A few months later, she was scheduled for a checkup. She was frightened that the tests might reveal a recurrence of this dreaded disease.

Many people suffer daily from attacks of fear and anxiety. The difference between the fear and anxiety is that specific reasons cause fear such as my mother's dread of cancer. Anxiety is a fear-like state of general agitation and insecurity whose source is not easily identifiable. Both can quickly destroy our equilibrium and adversely influence our well-being. In the short term, a panic attack can render a person dysfunctional. When it strikes, something quite ordinary like walking to the corner grocery store becomes a frightening task. In the longer term, fear and anxiety cause the fight-or-flight response to kick in and over time chronic stress can bring on disease.

Here are three suggestions to contend with fear and anxiety:

1) Meditate on a regular basis. At the Stress Reduction Clinic at the University of Massachusetts Medical Center, Jon Kabat-Zinn and his colleagues studied the effects of meditation on people who suffered from fear and anxiety attacks. They examined the levels of anxiety, depression, and panic in twenty-three people who were learning stress reduction techniques and meditation training. At the end of three months, Kabat-Zinn reported:

> *We found that both anxiety and depression dropped markedly in virtually every person in the study. So did the frequency and severity of their panic attacks. The three-month follow-up showed that they maintained their improvements after completion of the program. Most individuals were virtually free of panic attacks by the end of the follow-up period.*

2) In an emergency, begin abdominal breathing while focusing on the stomach area. I have found that the symptoms of an anxiety attack can be lessened by the following methods: 1) deep abdominal breathing to relax the body/mind and 2) focusing the mind's eye on a point just below my belly button. Apart from physical symptoms, my experience of fear is that thoughts and energy begin to fly fast and furious in every direction. By focusing attention to the mid-point of my body, I can contain and anchor this stampeding energy to my center in a physical and mental sense. If you can do this, the anxiety attack will probably subside in intensity. This technique is one way of using the art of "centering" for practical results.

1. A helpful hint is to place your hands, right on left, over your belly button as you breathe abdominally. This helps to focus your attention.
2. Then massage the stomach with gentle circles.

3) During meditation, be an objective observer of your fear. When you feel strong enough, experience your fear during the meditation. Do not push it away. There is often a good reason for feelings of fear. In my mother's case, it is an understandable fear of cancer, dying and death. By penetrating to the core source of your anxieties, you can begin to work with them and grow stronger and wiser. Fear can be a great teacher. But if you run or hide from your fears, they will follow you wherever you go and bedevil you like the perverbial schoolyard bully. "There is no terror in a bang," said Alfred Hitchcock, the master of suspense, "only in the anticipation of it."

Robert Smith, a well-known teacher of T'ai Chi, tells this story of Cheng Man Ch'ing, Smith's teacher. One day Professor Ch'ing was walking along a narrow mountain path when he met a tiger coming toward him. He knew that if he showed fear, the tiger would attack. While keeping eye contact with the tiger, he noticed a sapling growing next to him. Slowly, he bent the sapling toward the tiger's nose and held it there. The tiger sniffed it and shook his massive head. After a while, the tiger turned from his human prey and went down the mountain path, passing by Professor Cheng. Then, with the danger over, he began to shake. When the shaking passed, he continued on his journey.

Professor Cheng had learned to master his fear through meditation and the practice of martial arts. You can do the same. Meditation teaches the mind discipline and can make you the master of your destiny.

Coping with Pain

Looking directly at your own pain can be a frightening and unnerving experience. If you have looked into the mirror on a bad headache day and experienced the shock of seeing someone with whom you are barely acquainted staring back at you, then you know the terror of confronting your own pain. You can turn away from the mirror, but the image will remain with you. The thought might cross your mind: this is not the real me and this is not the me that I want to be. These kinds of thoughts are positive because they plant the seeds of change. The next step is absolutely crucial. You must want to do something about it. You must decide here and now that you are not going to be a victim. You must begin to make the appropriate changes in your life.

There are two sides of pain; the pain itself and one's attitude toward it. If the pain sufferer can confront the reality of his affliction, he may be able to alter his relationship to the pain. The way one thinks about pain often determines its role in his or her life. Our attitude can be a bigger obstacle to health than the actual pain itself. Fear and dread can touch off a snowball effect where what began as something small generates into an avalanche of suffering. In the example of migraine headaches, there is fear of how long the pain will last, will there be nausea, and panic over how one will be able to fulfill commitments. Strangely enough, in order to cope with one's pain, as Dr. Joan Borysenko observed, "You have to let go of trying to push it away." What is more, you can even learn to dance with your pain.

In T'ai Chi we have an exercise called push-hands where there is a dynamic interplay of two partners pushing and yielding with each other. Sometimes with beginners I take a strong rooted stance and ask them to push me away. Usually they cannot as I play the role of a pest who doggedly stays in their way. Then I tell them to dance with me, try to finesse me this way and that. Play with me instead of trying to dominate or suppress me. Usually there is a release of tension on their part. I may still be there but at least I am more fun and not the least bit overwhelming.

If pain is your pest, next time try

to finesse it. Play with its parameters. Try to breathe deeply and find the positions that lessen its intensity. This idea holds true from headache pain to the contractions of childbirth. During the giving birth of her first child, Naomi, one of my T'ai Chi students, described her process of working with pain this way:

> *You can react to pain as if it is something against you and it is trying to hurt you. Then you become hard and stiff. But if you relate to the pain as something that is a positive process, that's helping you, then you need not resist it. You can take those strong muscular contractions and you can make them yours. And that's like taking your opponent's aggression (in T'ai Chi) and turning it into your favor.*

Another way to think of pain is that it resembles a rebellious teenager. Trying to control or dominate your son or daughter will lead to immediate problems or ones that will express themselves in the future. Sending your son or daughter up to their rooms each time that they disobey you will soon become old hat. They will develop a tolerance to it and may even come to enjoy spending time alone in the room. Taking a painkiller all the time is something like sending your pain up to its room. Soon it will also become impervious to the effects of the medicine. As in the case of rebound headaches, the pain may even thrive on what once was the cure.

The Smile Meditation

Laughter is a key element in pursuing The Middle Path because it is the lusty music of health and sanity. It can take the edge off our seriousness or self importance. When we can poke fun at ourselves or at life, we reduce the possibility of taking extreme actions. A good laugh is often insightful as well as relaxing and is one reason why comedy is so popular throughout the world.

The Smile Meditation is one of my favorite exercises because it is good for body and soul. Dr. Bernie Siegel wrote that after a good laugh:

All the muscles are relaxed including the heart —
the pulse rate and blood pressure temporarily
decline. Psychologists have found that
<u>*muscle relaxation and anxiety cannot exist together....*</u>

When seriously ill, Norman Cousins prescribed for himself a "laugh therapy" that included watching comedies on video and reading humorous books. He credits this therapy for his complete recovery.

We have the expression, "to crack a smile." It suggests that someone's facial expression was frozen like a protective wall of stone and that a smile broke through his or her stern countenance. A smile or a good laugh relaxes and opens us up to others. We become more spontaneous. In a tense situation a well-told joke can melt the ice.

The Smile Meditation is easy to learn. Begin by sitting upright in a comfortable chair, close your eyes and breathe deeply. Focus on your breath for a while until you feel relaxed and ready.

In your mind's eye, recall a funny event that caused you to smile or laugh. It can be something that actually happened to you, a joke or a scene from a funny movie. Let yourself smile or laugh at the event.

My favorite humorous scene is the time we took my mother to visit a zoo. She is frightened of snakes. During our tour, she walked over to ask a question of a person who worked at the zoo. He was facing away from her. When my mother reached him, he turned around, holding a huge snake in his hands. She jumped about 10 feet backwards. I had never seen her move so fast. Afterwards a good laugh was had by all of us. I often use this scene in my smile meditations. As I am writing now and thinking of what happened to my mother, it brings a smile to my lips.

Be aware of how your mind and facial features relax as you begin to smile. Stay with that feeling and continue to breathe and relax. Try to strengthen the smile by returning to the event that caused it.

When the smile is strong, bring it to the rest of your body. Move the feeling of the smile from your face to your throat and chest. Let it settle in your heart. Let your heart smile with joy. Bring it to the rest of your organs: your lungs, liver, spleen and stomach. Let them also be joyful. Continue down the rest of your body until you reach the bottoms of your feet, stopping at the important places along the way.

Sometimes the pleasant feeling of the smile can be transformed into rays of light. Gradually fill your entire body with the smile, your arms, hands and shoulders. You can do it step by step as in the mind's eye relaxation meditation, the third exercise of Chapter V, or you can visualize it happening all at once.

From time to time, you may want to return to the funny event in order to reconnect with the experience or you may want to think of a different one. Then, when you are ready to finish, tell yourself to keep the smile for the rest of the day and night. Let the smile be in your dreams and in your relationship with other people. Let the good feeling of it suffuse your life and bring joy to you as you go about your daily affairs.

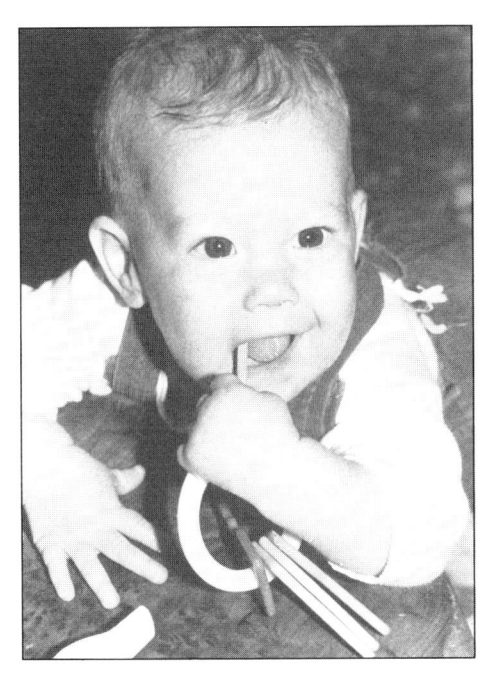

Special Needs:

Recently I taught a group of senior citizens the smile meditation. Usually I lead a meditation and exercise class with them, standing and sitting. On this day, they complained of being tired and did not want to do our normal routine. Conforming to their wishes, I led a sitting meditation. Then we did a few Ch'i Kung exercises loosely based on the exercises in Chapter VIII

I try to be creative with them and sensitive to their mood. So I decided to try the smile meditation. I was not sure whether they would be able to visualize or even understand what I meant. But I was wrong. The smile meditation worked beautifully. Afterwards, we shared our funny experiences and laughed together. It was one of the best classes I have ever conducted.

Chapter 8

Strengthening Your Ch'i:
Two Sets of Chinese Ch'i Kung

The Immortals of ancient days
While doing their breathing exercises,
Passed their time like dormant bears,
Looking about like owls,
Twitching and stretching their limbs and joints
In order to arrest the advance of old age.

Wu P'u on the Animal Forms of Ch'i Kung

Introduction

If you visit China and take an early morning stroll, you will encounter hundreds of people exercising in the parks. It is a stunning sight to see so many people, young and old, moving in such strange and unusual ways (at least to the untrained eyes of a Westerner). It might occur to you that you have stumbled onto a day camp for the slightly impaired and the happily insane. The rhythms of their movements are varied, sometimes slow and sometimes faster, without any apparent logic. Some of these early risers radiate an aura of something languid and ancient like the sleepy stretching of an animal on waking. Others may be doing the graceful, flowing postures of T'ai Chi. A few do not move at all, but stand still like statues in front of a tree. They are of course practicing Standing Meditation.

Despite first impressions, there is a rational explanation for their actions. These people are performing Ch'i Kung exercises, of which there are hundreds of varieties. Ch'i Kung traces its origins to the famous Chinese medical text, The Yellow Emperor's Classic of Internal Medicine (probably written about 1000 BCE). The Chinese words Ch'i Kung mean 'the developing of Ch'i skills.' According to Chinese medical theory, Ch'i is the internal energy or life-force of the body/mind. Traditionally the Chinese believe that if the Ch'i is not strong and balanced, then the body will suffer illness and eventual death. Hence, Ch'i Kung exercises were developed specifically to strengthen the Ch'i in order to maintain health.

If you were to engage a group of Ch'i Kung devotees in conversation, you would soon discover that they come from a wide variety of backgrounds. If you were to ask them why they are doing these exercises, they would explain that they are seeking to maintain health and lengthen their lives. They might also add that they enjoy doing Ch'i Kung in the fresh, early morning air.

These are similar reasons that a Westerner might give for jogging or swimming. However, for the most part, Easterners and Westerners view the relationship between exercise and health differently. A Westerner would argue that a good cardiovascular workout will keep the heart and all the organs fit and in good working order. In contrast, while not denying the value of cardiovascular exercise, the Ch'i Kung devotee believes that the most important reason for exercise is to harmonize the body's energy, that is to say, its Ch'i. This is best done, they believe, through gentle movement in coordination with concentrating the mind and the breath.

These ideas make sense when we think back on the nature of body/mind unity and the role of the relaxation response. Because Ch'i Kung emphasizes the integration of body, breath, and mind, it is a perfect tool to engage the relaxation response. Ch'i Kung, like meditation, helps the body/mind to find its natural balance. In addition, Ch'i Kung is practiced in a standing position with movement and breath, combining the qualities and benefits of exercise and meditation. Along with T'ai Chi, these ancient Chinese exercises represent the ultimate paradigm for maintaining and improving body/mind health.

Ch'i Kung is a valuable tool in combating stress and the ill effects of a sedentary lifestyle. For example, a student of mine who is in charge of the computer department of a large company often spends long hours in front of a computer screen. Occasionally, he will take a break to practice Ch'i Kung in the company's conference room. These body/mind exercises help him to feel better by re-focusing his awareness, relaxing his muscles and improving his body alignment. He returns to his work, refreshed and re-charged. He told me that sometimes after doing Ch'i Kung he views a recalcitrant problem in a new light that allows for its resolution.

A more dramatic example of Ch'i Kung's benefits occurred to another student of mine, a woman suffering from Multiple Sclerosis. Her lower left side was nearly immobile, and she had lost all sense of feeling in her left leg. After doing Standing Meditation and the Eight Pieces of Brocade, which we will learn in this chapter, she felt the bottom of her left foot for the first time in months. Moreover, she was able to put a substantial portion of her weight on it.

One way to understand what happened to this student is the Law of Transformation: **Consciousness>Energy>Material World.** By doing the Ch'i Kung exercises, her consciousness, that is, her concentration, produced Ch'i or internal energy which in turn affected her physical condition. A dialectic of thoughts, imagination and physical movement occurred and created a healing dynamic. This kind of transformation is available to everyone. It is a perfect example of using the mind to exercise the body.

The good news about Ch'i Kung exercises is that they are easy to learn and, in most cases, produce quick results. One famous Ch'i Kung therapist, a Chinese physician trained in both Western and traditional oriental medicine, stated that the most effective Ch'i Kung is simply to do Standing Meditation. From his experience, he had discovered that by doing less, Standing Meditation, he could achieve more. He added, however, that experience had also taught him to employ various forms of movement with his patients. The problem with standing, and apparently doing less, is that it bores most people.

This is easy to understand. There is a belief that, to achieve results, a person must be active. Westerners and many Chinese believe that the more vigorously a person exercises, the healthier he or she will be. Afterwards, one must feel tired, sweat a lot, and have sore muscle.

Clearly the attitude that one needs intense physical exercise to maintain health does not reflect the traditional wisdom of the East or even recent scientific findings in the West. There is a Chinese saying that sums up the purpose of Ch'i Kung: 'Find your center and you will be healed.' When you find your center, you have also found The Middle Path.

Weather permitting, it is best to practice Ch'i Kung out-of-doors, but one can also benefit from these exercises at home or in the office. The financial outlay is minimal, no special clothing or equipment is required. Any quiet space with proper ventilation will do. These ancient exercises are eminently practical while offering a healthy approach for nearly all people in every season of their lives. In short, Ch'i Kung is a gentle way to be strong.

Special Needs

Once you can do a few of these exercises and understand the general concept of movement and breath, you can then create your own Ch'i Kung exercise. It is possible to take the form of most living things and weave them into a Ch'i Kung exercise. In my classes with senior citizens, I ask them to think of one of their favorite things in the world. I begin the exercise with the image of a bird in flight, gently flapping my arms like the wings of a bird while sinking and rising with the movement. I coordinate the flapping with the breath. Then I ask them for a form of something close to their heart and a way of representing it with movement. One lady suggested a flower. The class moved their hands in concentric cirlces to represent the petals of a flower. I helped with the rhythm of the breath. Another lady chose the way her grandchildren wave to her. There are an infinite number of possibilities. Besides being fun, this form of creative Ch'i Kung makes the movement very personal.

All the Ch'i Kung exercises in this chapter are gentle and can be done sitting or standing. Simply modify them to meet your needs. If you can, begin by standing. If you tire, sit down and continue doing them. Remember, a key to The Middle Path is knowing yourself and not overdoing.

1st Exercise

The Eight Pieces of Brocade

The Chinese name for the 'Eight Pieces' is Ba Duan Jin. According to tradition, in the twelfth century Marshal Yueh Fei developed these exercises to improve the health of his soldiers. Brocade is a piece of cloth, usually silk, that is woven with intricate and colorful designs. The idea of the 'Eight Pieces of Brocade' is to weave the body/mind into a balanced picture of natural health so that the muscles are stronger, the limbs more supple, and the Ch'i flowing and balanced.

The 'Eight Pieces' represent a marriage between Ch'i Kung and calisthenics because they contain both the qualities of meditation and the physical effort of exercise. Although the outward movements are smooth and soft, they are performed with a degree of strain. But one should not overstrain. The 'Eight Pieces' are particularly beneficial in toning the arm and leg muscles, stretching the body, and improving posture. Its practitioners believe that the 'Eight Pieces' most important benefit is the overall strengthening of the immune system.

Preparation

Place your feet parallel, shoulder width apart and toes on the same line. From my experience, the direction or misdirection of the feet and the body often determine the level of one's focus. The knees should be slightly bent, not locked. The back is straight with the head over the spine as though being gently drawn upwards with a string. The arms hang comfortably along the sides of the body while the hands are open, fingers straight but without tension. The shoulders, chest, and stomach are relaxed downwards. (This is the opposite of standing at attention in the military with the chest protruding.) The eyes are open and alert. Focus your attention on doing these exercises correctly and on the inhaling and exhaling of the breath. Be sure to breathe abdominally. If unwanted thoughts intrude, gently bring your attention back to the breath and the exercises. Try to stay in the present moment, no matter what occurs with your thoughts or bodily sensations.

You are now ready to begin. The set of 'Eight Pieces' can be repeated several times if one so desires.

1. Holding Up the Sky

This exercise is particularly good for one's posture as well as strengthening the legs. It also opens up the lungs and allows for deeper breathing.

1. Breathe in – bring the fingers together and interlace them as the hands slowly rise up the front of the body. (Figure 1a)

Figure 1a

2. Breathe out – at chest level, the palms begin to turn outward and to face toward the sky, gradually stretching upward. Also begin to rise up on the toes. (Figure 1b)

3. Breathe in – the hands separate and begin to move down the sides of the body to the halfway point. (Figure 1c)

Figure 1b

4. Breathe out – the hands continue the rest of the way down.
5. Do this exercise 6 times.

Special needs: 'Holding up the sky' can be sitting down with the same breath and arm movements as above. If done standing, one need not rise onto the toes.

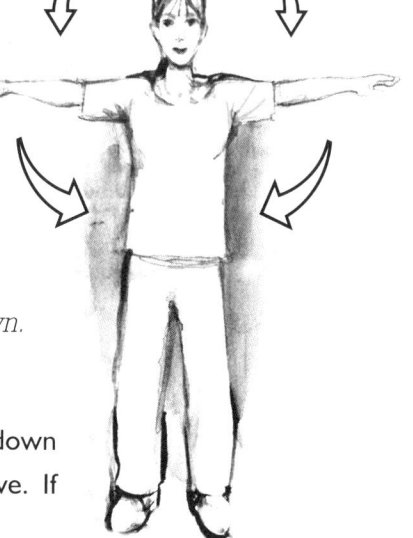

Figure 1c

2. Bending the Bow

This exercise is good for opening the lungs, expanding the chest and strengthening the thighs.

1. Breathe in – bring your hands to chest level and cross them, right hand to the outside, as the weight shifts to the right leg.(Figure 2a)

Before the weight shifts to left leg, form an archer's sight with the left hand (Figure 2c), and make a fist with the right hand and draw the bow.

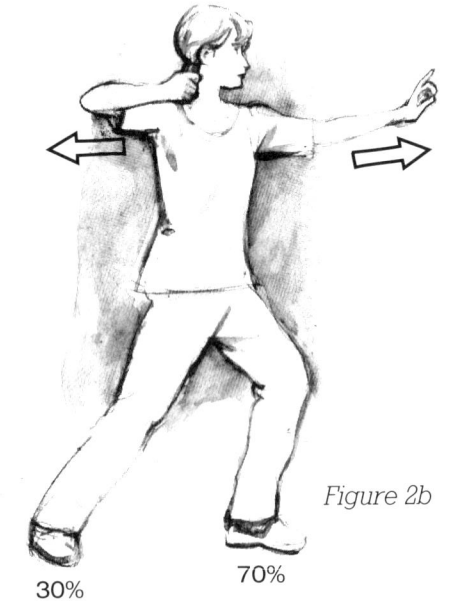

Figure 2c

80%   20%

Figure 2a

2. Breathe out – with the left leg, step to the left side, toes facing the side, and gradually shift the weight so that the left knee is over the toes and the right leg is almost straight. The left hand stretches to the left side and the right hand withdraws as if pulling on a bow string.

Figure 2b

30%   70%

3. Through the archer's sight, pick something in the distance and focus on it.
4. Breathe in – shift the weight to the right foot, step back to a parallel position with the left foot, as the hands drop down and up in a circular motion to a crossed position at chest level, the left hand to the outside. Form sight with right hand and a fist with left.
5. Breathe out – repeat step no. 2 to the right side.
6. Do each side a total of 3 times.

Strengthening Your Chi 111

Special Needs

This above exercise is not difficult to do physically. The problem for many students is remembering and coordinating the sequence of the exercise. Be patient and do it the best you can. The most important part is to pay attention to the breath and to focus through the sight between your thumb and index finger on something in the distance. It helps to form the sight and fist before you step out.

3. Touch the Earth and Sky

This exercise is designed to stimulate the spleen and the stomach. It also limbers up the lower back where you should feel it stretching.

1. Breathe in – raise the hands to chest level and cross them, the left hand to the outside. At the same time, sink down slightly into the knees. (Figure 3a)

2. Breathe out – turn the left hand and raise it with the palm upward, fingers together, pointing to the right and stretching up. The elbow is fully extended. Simultaneously the right hand pushes and stretches downward, fingers pointing forward. The weight has shifted mostly to the left leg and you are standing on the toes of the right leg. (Figure 3b)

3. Repeat to the other side.

4. Do this exercise 3 times on each side.

Figure 3a

90%
10%
Figure 3b

Special Needs

This exercise and the next one are easy to do. If you cannot stand, you can do them sitting.

4. Looking Back

This exercise is beneficial for neck pain from injury or disease, dizziness, and general fatigue.

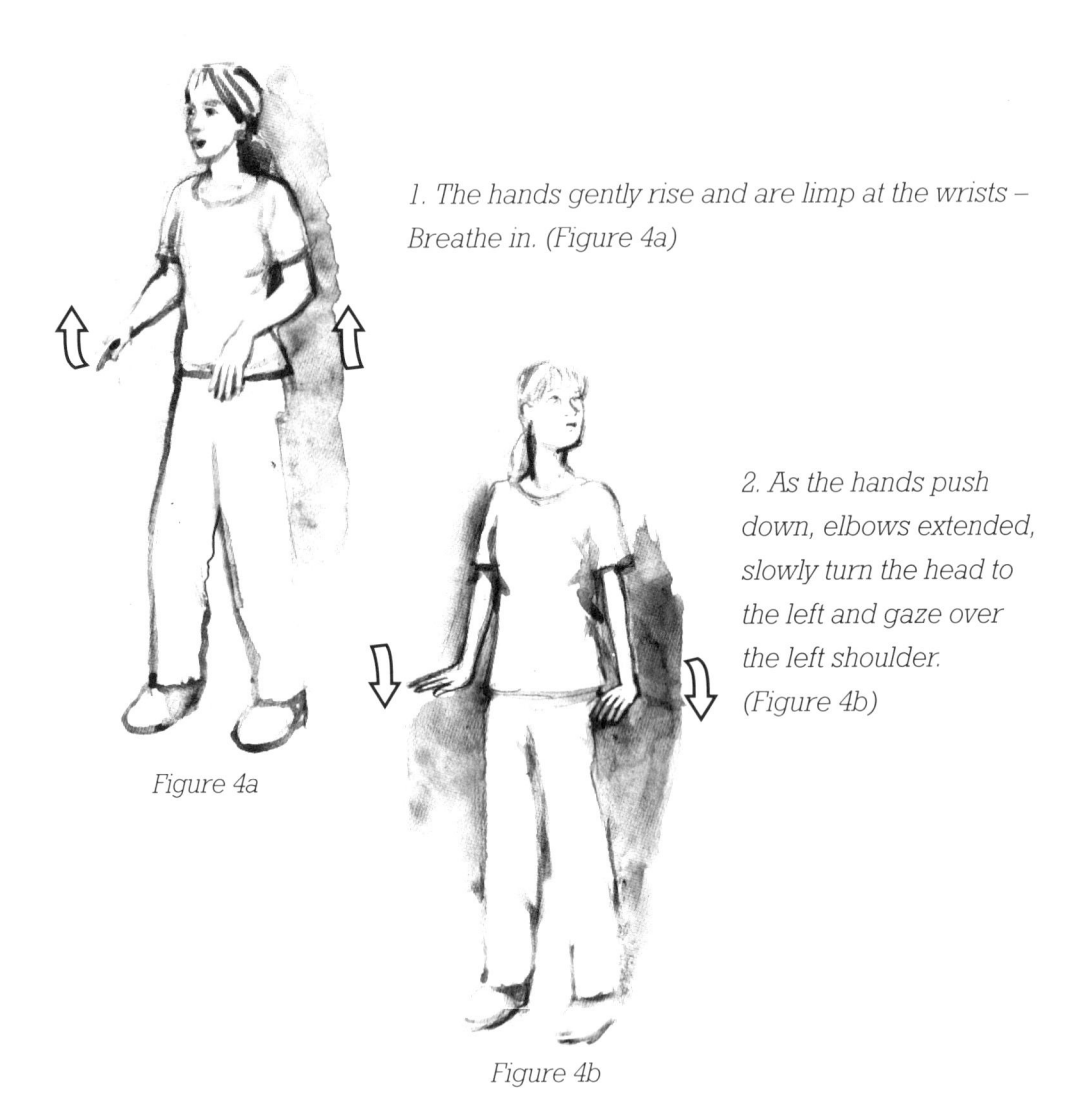

1. The hands gently rise and are limp at the wrists – Breathe in. (Figure 4a)

2. As the hands push down, elbows extended, slowly turn the head to the left and gaze over the left shoulder. (Figure 4b)

Figure 4a

Figure 4b

3. As you turn back to the center, raise the hands and allow the wrists to be limp, the same as Fig. 4a – Breathe in.
4. Repeat no. 2 to the right side.
5. Do this exercise 3 times on each side, for a total of 6.

5. Reaching for the Earth, Gazing at the Sky

This exercise helps to restore vitality to the kidneys and loosens a tight lower and upper back.

1. Breathe in – While standing upright, raise the hands to stomach level, fingers facing one another and palms up. (Figure 5a)

2. Breathe out – turn the hands over, fingers facing one another, and allow the body to relax down with gravity (be sure to relax your neck and bend the knees slightly). Try to touch the earth with the palms of parallel hands, the elbows extended. (Figure 5b)

Figure 5a

Figure 5b

3. Breathe in – raise body slowly and bring the hands to hips.

4. Breathe out – bend over backwards and gaze at the sky, hands on lower back. (Figure 5c)

5. Repeat this exercise 6 times.

Special needs

People with back problems should not do this exercise. Another possiblity is to moderately bend over and then back. I have an elderly student with back problems who follows this approach. I also have two students who suffer from vertigo, who cannot do this exercise. Bending over depends on the physical conditions of the individual.

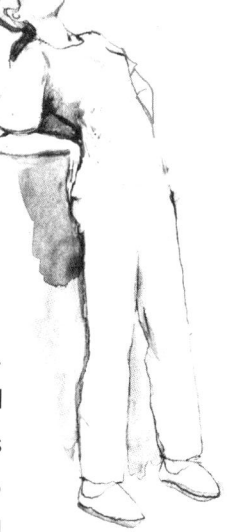

Figure 5c

6. Calming the Heart by Inclining to the Left and Right

This exercise is beneficial for the heart and alleviates mental disturbances such as insomnia and general nervousness.

1. Take a wider stance.
2. Breathe in – place the hands on waist. (Figure 6a)
3. Breathe out – let the body and head lean over to the left side naturally (do not force it down but defer to gravity) and allow the right hand to relax down, left hand remains on waist. The left knee receiving the majority of weight naturally bends slightly. (Figure 6b)

Figure 6a

4. Breathe in – raise the body to beginning position with both hands on hips.
5. Breathe out – repeat no. 3 to the right side.
6. Do this exercise 3 times on each side.

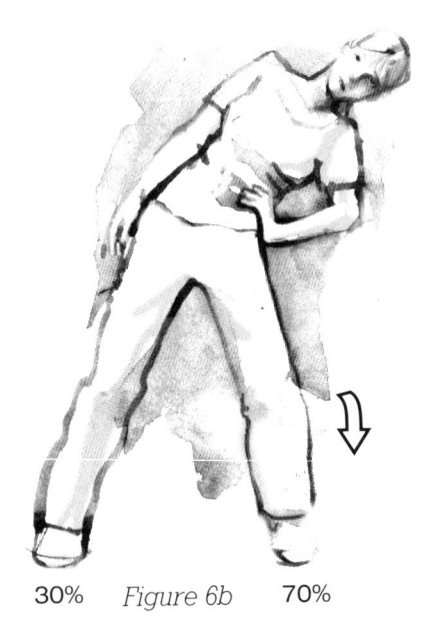

30%   *Figure 6b*   70%

Special needs

Bend ever so slightly. Be careful of putting too much weight on one leg. This exercise can also be done sitting.

7. Punching for Health

This exercise is good for general body strength, especially the legs. It also helps body coordination after one develops the proper rhythm between the waist, weight and fists.

1. Keep the wider stance, with bent knees.
2. Breathe in – raise hands to stomach level, palms up. (Figure 7a)
3. Breathe out – form fists and punch out with left fist. As the left fist fully extends, turn the fist a half turn to the right so that the fingers are parallel with the floor. Simultaneously the right hand forms into a fist and moves to the side of the waist, fingers pointing up. The waist turns to the right and the weight shifts to the right foot. Gaze over the left fist with intention. (Figure 7b)

Figure 7a

4. Breathe in – Open the fists and withdraw the left hand, fists in front of the stomach, as in Figure 7a.
5. Repeat no. 3 with the right fist striking out.
6. Do this exercise 3 times on each side.

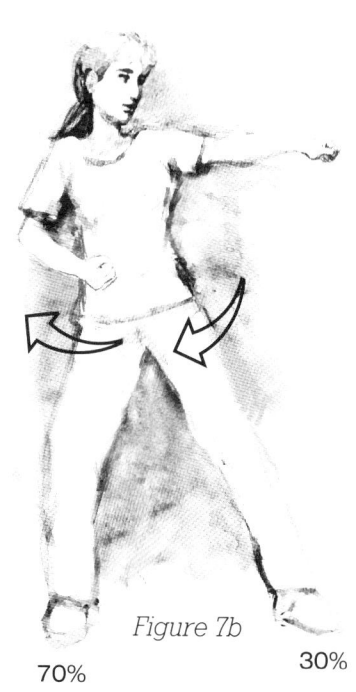

Figure 7b

70%   30%

Special Needs

Be careful of your knees when you turn the waist. Don't separate the legs too far. Don't worry too much about the coordination of the waist and weight in the beginning. It takes a while to get the hang of this exercise.

8. Dropping the Weight of the World

This exercise is known as a general cure for sickness. It also improves posture and strengthens the calf muscles.

1. Breathe in – rise up off the heels and lift the hands to the level of the chest, palms facing in. (Figure 8a)
2. Breathe out – drop on the heels and let the arms fall to the side. (Figure 8b)
3. Do this 6 times.

Figure 8a

Figure 8b

Special Needs

You need not rise onto your toes. Keep your feet flat on the ground. Then raise the body up with the inhale and let it slump a bit with the exhale.

2nd Exercise:

The Animal Forms

In China the close observation and the imitation of animal movements played an important part in the development of martial arts and Ch'i Kung. In Chinese medical theory, animals were viewed as being healthier than human beings. Animals lived naturally in the wild, which represented the ideal for many Chinese thinkers, especially the Taoists. Because animals survived on instincts and spontaneity, they were nature's examples of being in harmony with Tao. Certain animals, like the tiger, were also admired for their qualities of strength and courage.

Hua T'o (141-203 CE), the father of Chinese anaesthesiology, introduced the first known cohesive set of Ch'i Kung exercises called Tao Yin. He based these exercises on the movement of various animals: the bear, tiger, crane, deer, and monkey. He recommended that when a person feels ill, one of the best remedies is to breathe and perform the animal exercises.

Chinese medicine was predicated on the idea that the universe is a naturally harmonious, interrelated unity. Everything is connected to everything else. In the following set of Ch'i Kung, you will experience something of that unity. Five of the following six exercises link an internal human organ to a specific animal and to emitting a certain sound. Practitioners of Ch'i Kung believed that the characteristics of the animal and the vibrations of the emitted sound resonated together in a special way that stimulated healing for a particular bodily organ. For example, Chinese philosophy associated the element of fire with the heart. Thus, the fire-breathing dragon symbolized the animal that is connected to the heart. Moreover, the heart had certain emotions associated with it, for example, joy and laughter. The sound for the heart is a zesty uninhibited 'hawwwwww.'

The following chart gives you an idea of the way in which the Chinese viewed the universe as an interconnected unity. It is an abridged version and focuses on the qualities relating to the animal forms of Ch'i Kung.

	Heart	**Lungs**	**Spleen**	**Liver**	**Kidneys**
Animal:	dragon	tiger	deer	monkey	bear
Sound:	hawwww	ssss (hiss)	whooooo	shhhhhhh	chayyyyy
Element:	fire	metal	earth	wood	water
Emotion:	joy	sorrow	sympathy	anger	fear
Virtue:	faith	justice	fairness	kindness	gentleness
Season:	summer	autumn	Indian summer	spring	winter
Senses:	tongue	nose	mouth	eyes	ears
Taste:	bitter	pungent	neutral	sour	salty
Color:	red	white	gold/yellow	green	blue

On completing the following exercises, I often feel a deep sense of relaxation combined with a feeling of being energized and alert. They are the most powerful examples of Ch'i Kung I have yet experienced. The combination of movement, breath, and sound invigorate the body/mind while focusing on each organ initiates a thorough cleansing process that detoxifies the body. The sixth exercise of this set, which does not have an animal or sound, is simply called 'expelling the toxins.' The animal forms are a total body/mind experience, and probably unlike anything you have encountered before.

Preparation

When you do each of these following exercises, you should focus on and visualize the particular organ you want to strengthen. Bring the healing power of the breath into the organ. Let the breath circulate and cleanse the organ. Then exhale the bad or poisonous energy. The intrinsic healing power of these exercises depends on the conscious link of mind and body. Through visualization you can forge a stronger network of body/mind communication. Pay special attention to the pictures of the shape and location of each bodily organ in order to enhance your energy and healing.

The sounds are also very important. Do them in a place where you can bellow out a zesty uninhibited sound. Even if you find it difficult to connect the sound to the organ, the discharge of auditory energy amplifies the powerful effect of these exercises. The combination of sound and exhalation opens up blockages. The body's energy begins to flow effortlessly. In martial arts, a sound is often vented to enhance the explosive energy in, say, a punch or a kick.

The 'Animal Forms' are another fine example of the Law of Transformation in action: **Consciousness>Energy>Material** World. It is your consciousness, your intention, combined with actual doing of the animal forms that will maximize your health benefits.

We are now ready to begin. Stand with feet parallel, shoulder-width apart and toes on the same line. The body is relaxed, arms hanging at the sides, and the back and head alignment is straight using the image of the string. Eyes are open and focused straight ahead. Take a few deep breaths. Relax.

I. The Heart Exercise:

In wisdom literature worldwide, the heart plays a central role. In the Bible it can reflect anguish (Jer. 23:9), evil (Gen. 8:21), delight (1 Kings 8:66) and warmth (Ps. 39:4). The heart was also regarded as the fountain of wisdom and understanding. In Chinese medicine the heart was linked to the emotions of joy as well as wisdom and clear-thinking. We've all heard of someone who was wounded emotionally and 'died of a broken heart.'

A. Animal: Dragon

B. Sound: hawwwwww

C. Practice

1. Focus your mind's eye on your heart. (Figure 9a)

Figure 9a

2. Take a deep breath into your heart as you stretch your arms toward the sky, hands making a fist. (Figure 9b)

Figure 9b

3. Bend the knees and sink down as far you can. The elbows also drop down. You are still breathing in. (Figure 9c)

Figure 9c

Hawwwwwww

4. As you rise to a standing position with open hands and fists stretched to the sky, release the powerful sound Hawwwwwwwwww to the end of your air capacity. (Figure 9d)

5. Use your mind's eye, as you release the sound, to imagine the heart being cleaned with the air of the "Haw" sound.

Figure 9d

6. Then breathe abdominally three times. (Figure 9e)

7. Bend over and circle your fists repeatedly which causes your shoulders to roll. This frees up trapped energy in the shoulders and the upper spine area. At the same time alternately bend your knees which causes your lower back to open up. The movement of the knees releases trapped energy in the lower spine. This circling of the fists is done after each of the organ exercises and is an important part of this exercise. Do not leave it out! (Figure 9f)

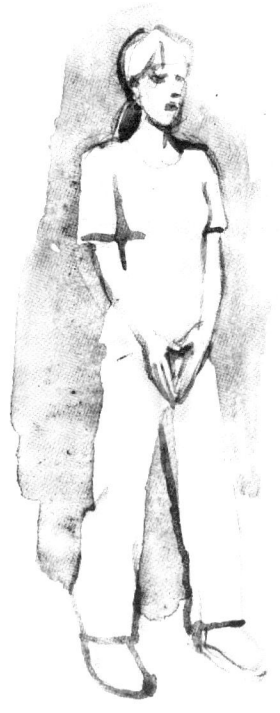

Figure 9e

8. If you can visualize colors easily, close your eyes and imagine that your heart has taken on a healthy color of red. Visualize your heart as a vital throbbing organ, pumping the blood throughout the body. It is an image of a strong powerful muscle.

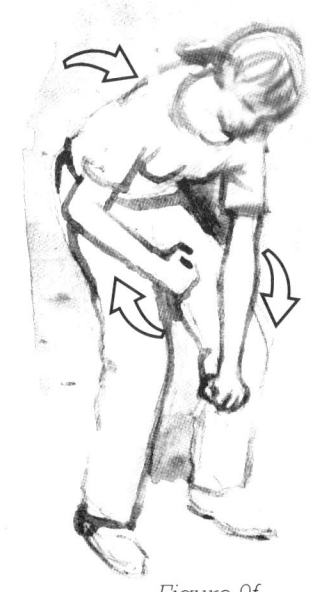

Figure 9f

II. The Lung Exercise:

In Chinese medicine excessive sadness or grief could weaken the lungs. The tiger exercise is particularly effective for eliminating recurring problems of flu, bronchitis and colds.

A. Animal: Tiger

B. Sound: SSSSSSSS
(like the hissing of a cat)

C. Practice

1. Focus your mind's eye on the lungs. (Figure 10a)
2. As you take in a deep breath, raise your hands toward the sky. (Figure 10b)

Figure 10a

Figure 10b

3. Sink down as far as you can, still taking in air and focusing on the lungs. The arms bend down at the elbows and hands form claws. (Figure 10c)

4. As you rise, release the hissing sssss sound of a cat in one slow and even breath. The claws stretch straight out from the chest. (To make the hissing sound, let the teeth gently meet and slightly separate the lips.) (Figure 10d)

5. Imagine that you are cleaning out the hot heavy energy in the lungs as you exhale the air with the sound. Replace it with the cool fresh air. (Try to do this exercise outside in a park or in a forest.)

Figure 10c

6. Breathe abdominally three times.
7. Repeat the 'rolling of the fists' from above. (Repeat of figure 9e & 9f, pg. 121)
8. Breathe and relax. Try to feel the changes occurring in your body.
9. If visualization comes easily to you, imagine a pure white or golden light filling your lungs. Try to feel this healthy energy permeating your lungs with each breath.

Figure 10d

III. The Spleen Exercise:

The spleen filters out foreign intruders and old red blood cells from the blood. It also produces certain types of white blood cells. A healthy spleen is a crucial link in a well functioning immune system. Interestingly, the Talmud speaks of the spleen as the source of laughter. (Brakhot 61b). We know that laughter and joy can strengthen the system as in the example of Norman Cousins who healed himself with laughter therapy. The spleen exercise is helpful for problems of indigestion, nausea and diarrhea.

A. Animal: deer

B. Sound: Whooooooo

C. Practice

*1. Focus on the spleen.
(Figure 11a)*

Figure 11a

Strengthening Your Chi 125

2. Breathe in deeply to the spleen and sink down, the left hand facing down at the level of the spleen, the right hand facing palm up above the head. (Figure 11b)

3. Turn the body to the left and make the whooo sound. (Figure 11c)

4. Hold the posture of the body, still turned to the left and breathe in deeply.

5. As you turn back to the center, breathe out.

6. At the center position, breathe in deeply as you switch the hands, the right to about the height of the spleen and the left hand facing palm up over the head.

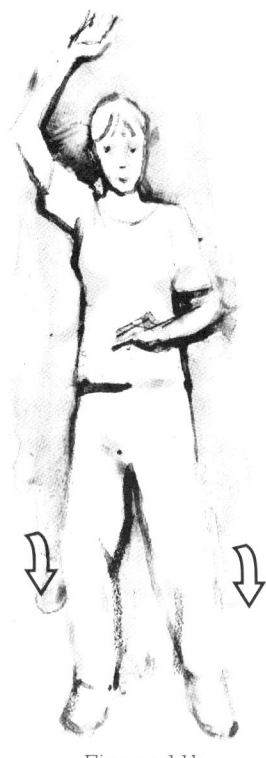

Figure 11b

7. Turn to the right, breathe out, and make the Whoooo sound (repeating no. 3 to the right side)

8. Hold the posture of the body being turned to the right and breathe in deeply.

9. As you turn back to the center, breathe out.

10. Stand and breathe in deeply 3 times.

11. Roll the fists.

12. Stand and place your hands on your spleen as in Figure 11a. With your mind's eye, breathe a gentle golden light into the spleen. Do this for a few breaths.

Whoooooooo

30%   70%

Figure 11c

IV. The Liver Exercise:

Among its many functions, the liver neutralizes harmful substances from the intestine. This exercise detoxifies the liver and prevents it from being overwhelmed by these poisons.

Ancient wisdom held that an unhealthy liver produces negative emotions. In the Bible the liver was known as the seat of anger. Similarly, in Chinese medical theory an imbalance of liver energy produced anger. On the other hand, a healthy liver harmonizes the emotions and reduces negative feelings.

A. Animal: monkey

B. Sound: Shhhhhhh

C. Practice

1. Focus on the liver.
(Figure 12a)

Figure 12a

Strengthening Your Chi 127

2. Breathe in deeply as the hands form gentle fists. They circle up and out from the sides of the body. (Figure 12b)

3. Still breathing in, bring the right fist directly over the liver and the left fist to same height as the right one on the left side of the body. (Figure 12c)

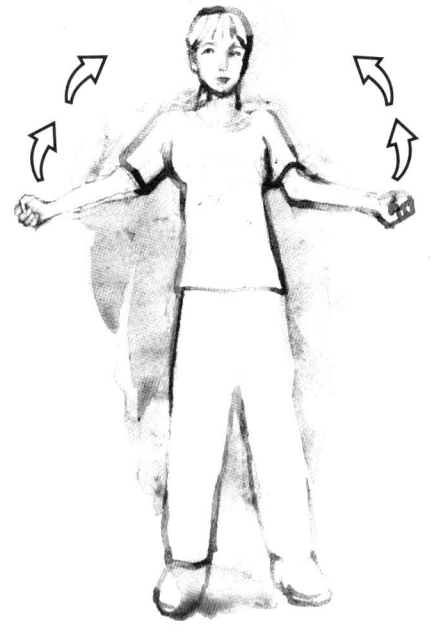

Figure 12b

4. The head is facing down and the body leaning slightly forward.

5. Release a powerful Shhhhhhh sound as though you were emphatically asking someone to be quiet.

6. Stand and breathe 3 times.

7. Roll the fists.

8. Cover the liver with your hands and visualize a soft healing green color, like the Spring grass of the fields, filling it.

Figure 12c

V. The Kidney Exercise:

This exercise is especially good for back pain and urinary problems. It is very important to detoxify the kidneys because they remove waste products from the blood and can create disease when overloaded.

A. Animal: bear

B. Sound: Chayyyyyyy
   (ch as in chair with a long 'A' sound)

C. Practice

1. Focus on the kidneys. (Figure 13a)
2. Because the bear is big and close to the ground, take a wider stance and sink down. (Figure 13b)

Figure 13a

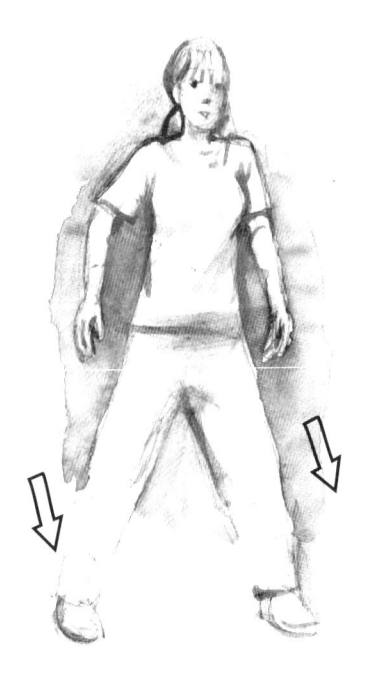

Figure 13b

Strengthening Your Chi   129

Figure 13c

3. As you breathe in deeply, circle your arms and gentle fists up and away from the body. (Figure 13c)

4. Place them just below the belly button, the level of the bladder.

5. Breathe out, releasing the powerful sound chayyyyyyy. (Figure 13d)

6. Stand and breathe 3 times.

7. Roll the fists.

8. Stand and place your hands on the lower tan tien. Focus on your kidneys and visualize the color blue or dark blue, the hue of the ocean. Breathe this color into the kidneys, without the sound. (Fig. 13d)

Figure 13d

VI. Expelling the body's toxins:

This exercise cleans out the entire body with each breath while the previous animal forms focus on specific organs. There is no animal or sound.

Figure 14a

A. Practice

1. After the bear exercise, return to a normal stance.
2. As you take a deep breath, bring the hands up to chest level, palms facing up. (Figure 14a)

3. As you bring the arms back, direct them toward the back corners. This all happens on the inhale. (Figure 14b)

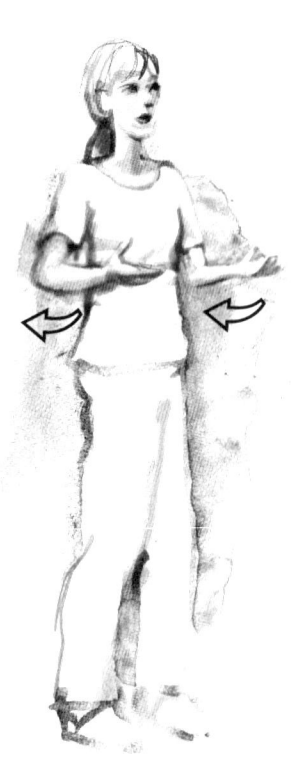

Figure 14b

Strengthening Your Chi 131

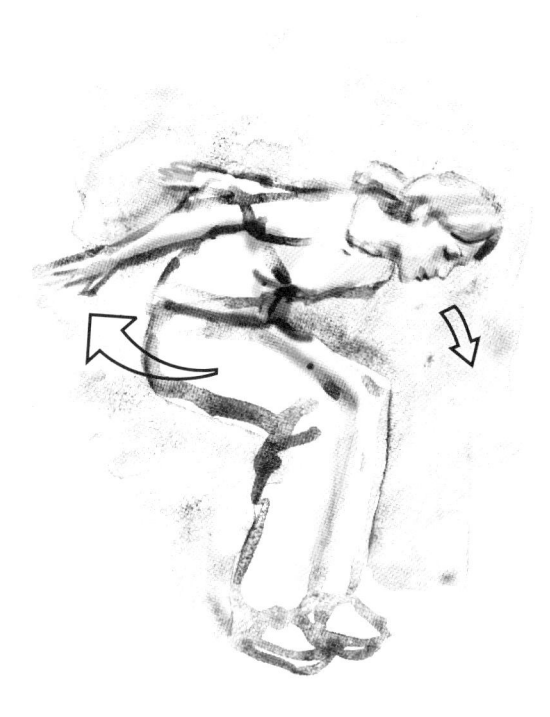

Figure 14c

4. As you breathe out, bend the knees and roll the body over so that the front of your torso is parallel to the floor. Your head is facing toward the ground. At the same time swing the arms back and stretch out like the wings of a jet plane. (Figure 14c)

5. Then breathe in as the body stands, and repeat the instructions of no. 3 & 4.

6. Do this exercise 9 times.

7. When you breathe in, imagine that fresh air is cleaning out your entire body. When you breathe out, expel all the toxins and direct them into the ground. The idea is that the earth absorbs these toxins and neutralizes them in the same way that it recycles animal waste products.

8. If you wish, you can breathe into your body the healing color of golden light or whatever color your preference might be. This can help with the detoxification process.

Helpful Hints

1. You can practice the animal forms at any time during the day or night. You can also use them as a warm-up or a warm-down for gentle exercises like T'ai Chi or for vigorous aerobic exercises.

2. Follow the sequence in these exercises. There is a logic to it. By energizing the heart and lungs first, it is then more effective to detoxify the spleen, liver and kidneys.

3. If you have a problem with one or more of these organs, repeat the exercise for it several times.

4. The act of focusing on and visualizing each organ is very important. The key to effective healing in Ch'i Kung is to mobilize the body/mind to work in perfect harmony. You also develop a sensitivity as to how well your body is functioning internally.

5. Be sure to breathe deeply and fully into the organ being focused on.

6. If you can, use the color visualization that corresponds to each organ. Certain colors like white radiate a feeling of cleanliness and well-being. Certain colors like red and blue can lift one's spirits. The correlation of bodily organs and color evolved over thousands of years of the Chinese historical experience.

7. Another possibility that you can add later is to end with the smile meditation. After you finish rolling the fists or expelling the toxins, simply think of something that makes you happy and smile down into the organ or fill up the entire body with good feelings.

The author teaching a Ch'i Kung class

Summary

Ch'i Kung is practiced all over China. Most hospitals, including those with a Western orientation, have recommended classes in Ch'i Kung. Research in China has demonstrated that Ch'i Kung exercises can help cancer patients cope with the unpleasant side effects of chemotherapy. In the West many pain and stress reduction clinics utilize Ch'i Kung in their programs. The gentle forms of Ch'i Kung are suitable for those who are too ill to do vigorous exercise or those with physical disabilities. Healing is an art that each one of us can participate in. We simply have to open up to our own potential. A famous Ch'i Kung teacher said that our healing capacity is limited only by the limitations of our imagination.

Afterword

Ultimately the question we must ask ourselves is: "What kind of life do I want for myself, my family and my community?" We have tremendous power at our finger tips. We can scan a person's body for illness with powerful machines or send people into outer space with an astounding array of complex technology. But what about inner space? Our body/minds are perhaps the most complex creation on the face of the earth. The brain's natural intelligence is the vanguard of millions of years of evolution. From a religious perspective, we are the vessels that contain the image of God. Through our natural inborn abilities, it is within our reach to change the course of our lives for the better. We need only to tap into it. When we do, we are using the mind to exercise the body. The paradox is that *less* only appears to be little on the surface. When we engage the power of the mind, *less* becomes more.

Our body/mind is like a large company, a concern of flesh and blood, that requires the resourceful leadership of a wise and perceptive chairperson of the board. You are that person! While most of the day-to-day operations of your body/mind run on delegated authority, your influence is crucial in establishing the ambiance as well as the vision. The professionals you might consult on health matters work for you and not the other way around. The key to wellness and well-being lies in your hands through the choices you make and the will to carry them through to the end.

Also Available

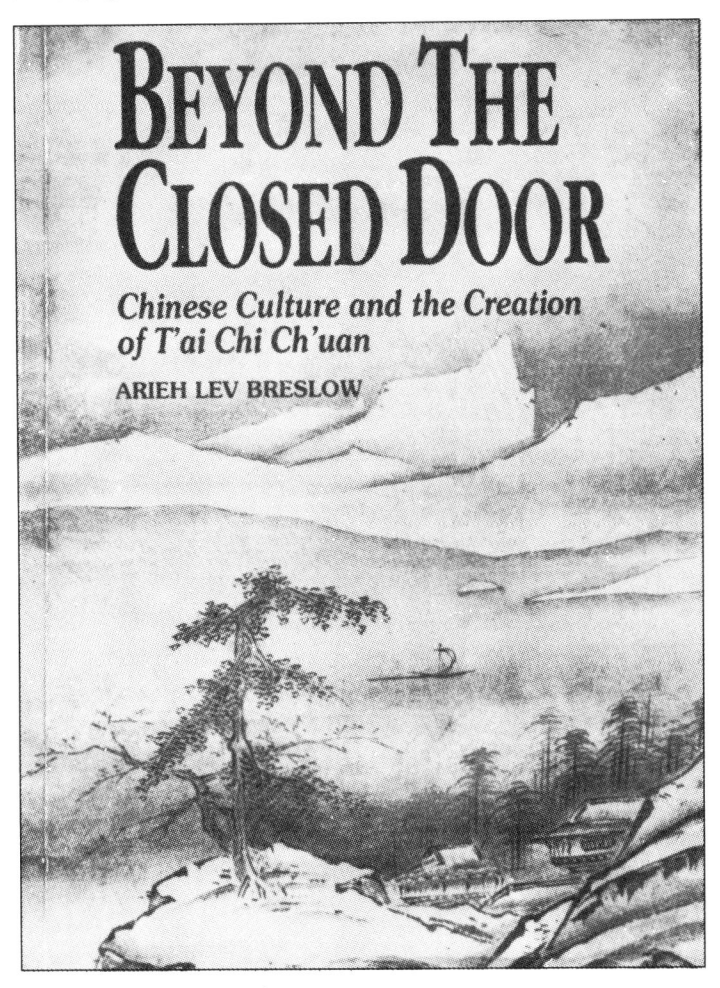

BEYOND THE CLOSED DOOR

Chinese Culture and the Creation of T'ai Chi Ch'uan

by Arieh Lev Breslow
Softcover, 397 pp.

Price $19.95

"This isn't just another T'ai Chi book: it examines the Chinese culture and traditions which have fostered T'ai Chi, considering Taoist thought, the origins and form of T'ai Chi, and the special challenges of it's principles."
— The Bookwatch, Reviewers Choice

"...it can be read and re-read on many levels; a well-written introduction to Chinese history and philosophy; a handbook of preliminary techniques in meditation; a guide to one of the oldest and most successful martial arts."
— The Jerusalem Post Magazine

"Beyond The Closed Door succeeds in introducing the mysteries of Chinese thought and culture, drawing together a vast array of sources, and piecing together the Chinese world view in a way that is intelligible to Westerners."
— Journal of Asian Martial Arts, 1996

The Middle Path Video

The Middle Path Video contains "A Warmup for the Middle Path," "The Eight Pieces of Brocade," and "The Animal Forms."

Available in NTSC and PAL modes.
Approximate running time, 1 hr.
Price $39.95.

The Middle Path Cassette

The Middle Path cassette contains instructions on how to meditate and guidance through several of the meditations in *When Less is More*.

Approximate running time, 1 hr.
Price $10.95.

Order Form

Payment

Payment is required in US dollars, or the equivalent in British Pound Sterling or the Euro, or by international money order in either of those two currencies.

When Less is More – book price: $19.95

Postage and handling

Video, *Beyond the Closed Door* or *When Less is More* – by surface $3.50, by air $5.00. Add $2.00 for each additional item.

Cassette alone – by surface $2.00, by air $3.50

Surface mail takes up to 12 weeks. Airmail within two weeks.

Quantity	Title	Unit price	Total
		Postage and handling charge	
		TOTAL	

For video, circle one:
Pal   or   NTSC

Check or money order payable to:　　**Ship to:**
Almond Blossom Press　　Name: _____
P.O. Box 10600　　Address: _____
Jerusalem, Israel　　City: _____ State: _____
Tel: 972-2-9933394　　Zip: _____

For book sales and workshops only, call: (no country prefix necessary)
In US: 1-877-209-2937 **In Canada:** 1-877-531-9791 **In UK:** 0-800-917-0021

Middle Path Workshops

Mr. Breslow offers workshops that:
1. Focus in depth on the ideas, meditations and exercises in "When Less is More."

2. Develop a practical framework of exercise for those with special needs. This workshop includes methods for teaching special needs students.

3. Teach several forms of Chi Kung, the principles of T'ai Chi and an introduction to the art of pushhands.

For details: 972-2-9933394, Fax: 972-2-9933459
Address: P.O.Box 10600, Jerusalem, Israel